ultimate
BOOK OF
baby knits

DEBBIE BLISS

Quadrille
PUBLISHING

THE ultimate BOOK OF baby knits

Debbie Bliss's favourite 50 patterns for babies and toddlers

DEBBIE BLISS

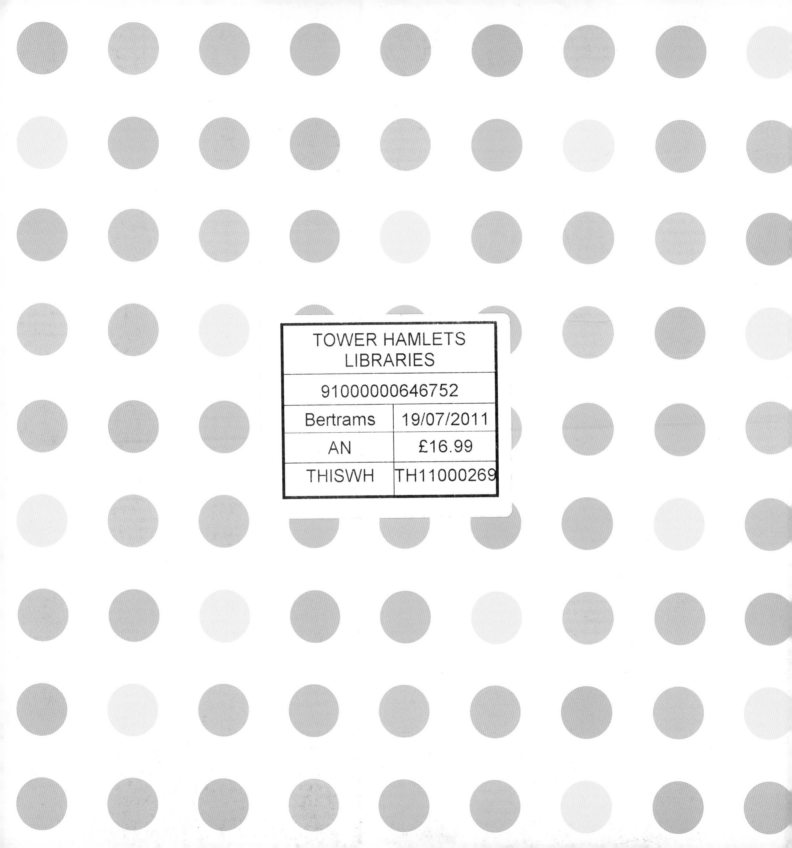

introduction

Throughout my years as a hand-knitter I have enjoyed dreaming up designs for both adults and children, yet there is something very special about creating hand-knits for babies. I gain huge satisfaction from every stage of putting a collection of baby knits together: from the initial sketches – when something sparks that first design idea – and selecting colourways, through swatching yarns and refining shapes to arriving at the finished garments and seeing them photographed on the children – the culmination of all that work.

At a time when so much of the clothes available for children are mass produced, the feelgood factor of either giving or receiving a hand-knitted baby garment is pretty hard to beat. The sheer joy of the recipient is matched by the warm satisfaction of the knitter. And for a beginner, the size of a baby

knit means that you can quickly see your project grow and take shape and, at the same time, practice any new techniques on a relatively small scale.

Designing for babies is very different from designing for men and women. Although style is equally important to all hand-knit designs, practicality and comfort also have to play an essential part in childrenswear. I tend to create jackets and cardigans rather than sweaters for tiny babies because as they cannot sit up at that stage it can be difficult to put garments on without causing them discomfort. When I do design a sweater for a baby, I incorporate a design feature such as an envelope neck or shoulder buttons so that the garment can be easily pulled over a baby's head.

Fibre content is paramount when choosing a yarn. Not only should it be soft against a baby's skin but it must

also be safe to wear. Yarns such as angora, alpaca and mohair have long, detachable fibres and are not suitable for babywear. All the yarns from my ranges included in this book have been chosen because they are baby-friendly, with extra-fine merino wools, cashmere blends and cotton mixes – all of which are machine washable but soft and gentle against young skin.

In putting together **The Ultimate Book of Baby Knits** I have selected my favourite fifty designs from three of my previous books – Simply Baby, Essential Baby and Blankets, Bears and Bootees. There are plenty of designs to choose from – classic cardigans and enveloping wraps to cosy hats and cute toys – suited to a range of knitting skills, but most are simple knits reflecting a new life-balance when nurturing may well take over from knitting.

knitting
basics

yarns

types of yarns

When choosing a yarn for babies or children, it is essential that you work with a fibre that is soft and gentle against a baby's skin. Babies are not able to tell you if a collar is rough against their neck or if cuffs are irritating their wrists, and as older children are often more used to the lightweight freedom of fleeces, they can be resistant to hand-knits that they may consider scratchy and uncomfortable.

The yarns I have chosen for the patterns in this book are cashmere combined with either cotton or merino wool, giving softness and durability, a pure cotton and an extra fine merino. Although they create fabrics that are sumptuously soft to wear, most importantly all these yarns are machine washable.

When knitting a garment, wherever possible try to buy the yarn stated in the pattern. All these designs have been created with a specific yarn in mind: the Hooded Jacket is worked in a softer yarn to gently frame a baby's face, whilst the Roll Edge Jacket is made in a natural cotton to give it the necessary sturdiness to maintain its shape – a floppier fibre or a synthetic yarn would create a limp fabric. From an aesthetic point of view, the clarity of a subtle stitch pattern may be lost if a garment is knitted in an inferior yarn.

However, there may be occasions when a knitter needs to substitute a yarn – if there is an allergy to wool, for example – and so the following is a guideline to making the most informed choices.

Always buy a yarn that is the same weight as that given in the pattern: replace a double knitting with a double knitting, for example, and check that the tension of both yarns is the same.

Where you are substituting a different fibre, be aware of the design. A cable pattern knitted in cotton when worked in wool will pull in because of the greater elasticity of the yarn and so the fabric will become narrower; this will alter the proportions of the garment.

Check the metreage of the yarn. Yarns that weigh the same may have different lengths in the ball or hank, so you may need to buy more or less yarn.

Here are descriptions of my yarns and a guide to their weights and types:

Debbie Bliss baby cashmerino:
A lightweight yarn between a 4ply and a double knitting.
55% merino wool, 33% microfibre, 12% cashmere.
Approximately 125m/50g ball.
Debbie Bliss cashmerino aran:
55% merino wool, 33% microfibre, 12% cashmere.
Approximately 90m/50g ball.
Debbie Bliss cashmerino double knitting:
55% merino wool, 33% microfibre, 12% cashmere.
Approximately 110m/50g ball.

Debbie Bliss Bella:
85% cotton, 10% silk, 5% cashmere.
Approximately 95m/50g ball.
Debbie Bliss cotton double knitting:
100% cotton.
Approximately 84m/50g ball.

buying yarn

The ball band on the yarn will carry all the essential information you need as to tension, needle size, weight and metreage. Importantly it will also have the dye lot. Yarns are dyed in batches or lots, which can vary considerably. As your retailer may not have the same dye lot later on, buy all your yarn for a project at the same time. If you know that sometimes you use more yarn than that quoted in the pattern, buy extra. If it is not possible to buy all the yarn you need with the same dye lot, use the different ones where it will not show as much – on a neck or border for example – as a change of dye lot across a main piece will most likely show.

It is also a good idea at the time of buying the yarn to check the pattern and make sure that you already have the needles you will require. If not, buy them now, as it will save a lot of frustration when you get home.

garmentcare

Taking care of your hand-knits is important because you want them to look good for as long as possible. Correct washing is particularly important for baby garments as they need to be washed often.

Check the ball band on the yarn for washing instructions to see whether the yarn is hand or machine washable, and if it is the latter, at what temperature it should be washed.

Most hand-knits should be dried flat on an absorbent cloth, such as a towel, to soak up any moisture. Laying them flat in this way gives you an opportunity to pat the garment back into shape if it has become pulled around in the washing machine. Even if you are in a hurry, do not be tempted to dry your knits near a direct heat source, such as a radiator.

As baby garments are small, you may prefer to hand wash them. Use a washing agent that is specifically designed for knitwear as this will be kinder to the fabric. Use warm rather than hot water and handle the garment gently without rubbing or wringing. Let the water out of the basin and then gently squeeze out the excess water. Do not lift out a water-logged knit as the weight of the water will pull it out of shape. You may need to remove more moisture by rolling it in a towel. Dry flat as before.

techniques

cast on

slip-knot

Your first step when beginning to knit is to work a foundation row called a cast-on. Without this row you cannot begin to knit.

There are several methods of casting on, each can be suited to a particular purpose or is chosen because the knitter feels comfortable with that particular technique. The two examples shown here are the ones I have found to be the most popular, the thumb and the cable methods.

In order to work a cast-on edge, you must first make a slip-knot.

1 Wind the yarn around the fingers on your left hand to make a circle of yarn as shown above. With the knitting needle, pull a loop of the yarn attached to the ball through the yarn circle on your fingers.

2 Pull both ends of the yarn to tighten the slip-knot on the knitting needle. You are now ready to begin, using either of the following cast-on techniques.

cast on

thumb cast-on

1 Make a slip-knot as shown on page 15, leaving a long tail. With the slip-knot on the needle in your right hand and the yarn that comes from the ball over your index finger, wrap the tail end of the yarn over your left thumb from front to back, holding the yarn in your palm with your fingers.

2 Insert the knitting needle upwards through the yarn loop on your left thumb.

The thumb cast-on is a one needle method that produces a flexible edge, which makes it particularly useful when using non-elastic yarns such as cotton. The 'give' in it also makes it a good one to use where the edge will turn back, as on the duffel coat (see page 68).

Unlike two-needle methods you are working toward the yarn end, which means you have to predict the length you need to cast on the required amount of stitches, otherwise you may find you do not have enough yarn to complete the last few stitches and have to start all over again. If unsure, always allow for more yarn than you think you need as you can use what is left over for sewing up.

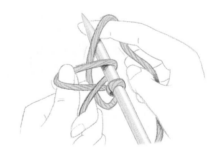

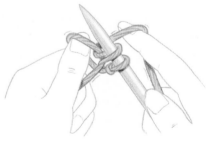

3 With the right index finger, wrap the yarn from the ball up and over the point of the knitting needle.

4 Draw the yarn through the loop on your thumb to form a new stitch on the knitting needle. Then, let the yarn loop slip off your left thumb and pull the loose end to tighten up the stitch. Repeat these steps until the required number of stitches have been cast on.

cable cast-on

1 Make a slip-knot as shown on page 15. Hold the knitting needle with the slip-knot in your left hand and insert the right-hand needle from left to right and from front to back through the slip-knot. Wrap the yarn from the ball up and over the point of the right-hand needle as shown.

2 With the right-hand needle, draw a loop through the slip-knot to make a new stitch. Do not drop the stitch from the left-hand needle, but instead slip the new stitch onto the left-hand needle as shown.

The cable cast-on method uses two needles and is particularly good for ribbed edges, as it provides a sturdy, but still elastic, edge. As you need to insert the needle between the stitches and pull the yarn through to create another stitch make sure that you do not make the new stitch too tight. The cable method is one of the most widely used cast-ons.

3 Next, insert the right-hand needle between the two stitches on the left-hand needle and wrap the yarn around the point of the right-hand needle.

4 Pull the yarn through to make a new stitch, and then place the new stitch on the left-hand needle, as before. Repeat the last two steps until the required number of stitches have been cast on.

knit

The knit and purl stitches form the basis of almost all knitted fabrics. The knit stitch is the easiest to learn and is the first stitch you will create. When worked continuously it forms a reversible fabric called garter stitch. You can recognise garter stitch by the horizontal ridges formed at the top of the knitted loops.

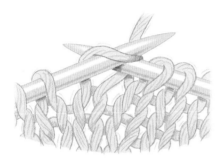

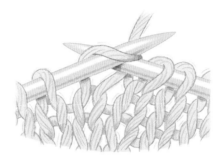

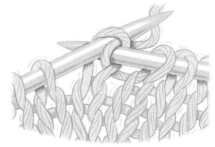

1 With the cast-on stitches on the needle in your left hand, insert the right-hand needle from left to right and from front to back through the first cast-on stitch.

2 Take the yarn from the ball on your index finger (the working yarn) around the point of the right-hand needle.

3 Draw the right-hand needle and yarn through the stitch, thus forming a new stitch on the right-hand needle, and at the same time slip the original stitch off the left-hand needle. Repeat these steps until all the stitches from the left-hand needle have been worked. One knit row has now been completed.

&purl

After the knit stitch you will move on to the purl stitch. If the purl stitch is worked continuously, it forms the same fabric as garter stitch. However, if purl rows and knit rows are worked alternately, they create stocking stitch, which is the most widely used knitted fabric.

  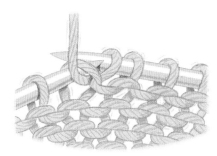

1 With the yarn to the front of the work, insert the right-hand needle from the right to the left into the front of the first stitch on the left-hand needle.

2 Then take the yarn from the ball on your index finger (the working yarn) around the point of the right-hand needle.

3 Draw the right-hand needle and the yarn through the stitch, thus forming a new stitch on the right-hand needle, and at the same time slip the original stitch off the left-hand needle. Repeat these steps until all the stitches have been worked. One purl row has now been completed.

increase

increase one

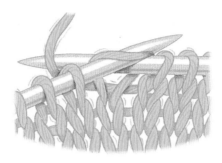 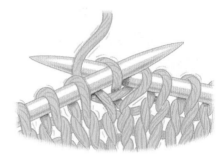

1 Insert the right-hand needle into the front of the next stitch, then knit the stitch but leave it on the left-hand needle.

2 Insert the right-hand needle into the back of the same stitch and knit it. Then slip the original stitch off the needle. Now you have made an extra stitch on the right-hand needle.

make one

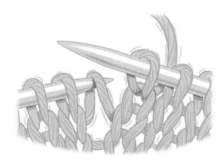 

1 Insert the left-hand needle from front to back under the horizontal strand between the stitch just worked on the right-hand needle and the first stitch on the left-hand needle.

2 Knit into the back of the loop to twist it, and to prevent a hole. Drop the strand from the left-hand needle. This forms a new stitch on the right-hand needle.

Increases are used to add to the width of the knitted fabric by creating more stitches. They are worked, for example, when shaping sleeves up the length of the arm or when additional stitches are needed after a ribbed welt. Some increases are invisible, while others are worked away from the edge of the work and are meant to be seen in order to give decorative detail. Most knitting patterns will tell you which type of increase to make.

yarn over

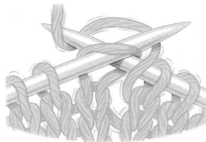

yarn over between knit stitches
Bring the yarn forward between
the two needles, from the back to
the front of the work. Taking the
yarn over the right-hand needle
to do so, knit the next stitch.

yarn over between purl stitches
Bring the yarn over the right-hand
needle to the back, then between the
two needles to the front. Then purl
the next stitch.

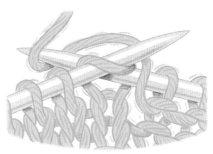

yarn over between a purl and a knit
Take the yarn from the front over
the right-hand needle to the back.
Then knit the next stitch.

yarn over between a knit and a purl
Bring the yarn forward between the
two needles from the back to the front
of the work, and take it over the top
of the right-hand needle to the back
again and then forward between the
needles. Then purl the next stitch.

cast off

Casting off is used to finish off your knitted piece so that the stitches don't unravel. It is also used to decrease more than one stitch at a time, such as when shaping armholes, neckbands, and buttonholes. It is important that a cast-off is firm but elastic, particularly when you are casting off around a neckband, to ensure that it can be pulled easily over the head. Unless told otherwise, cast off in the pattern used in the piece.

knit cast-off

 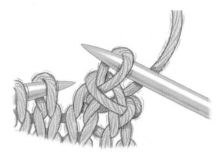

1 Knit two stitches. Insert the left-hand needle into the first stitch knitted on the right-hand needle and lift this stitch over the second stitch and off the right-hand needle.

2 One stitch is now on the right-hand needle. Knit the next stitch. Repeat the first step until all the stitches have been cast off. Pull the yarn through the last stitch to fasten off.

purl cast-off

1 Purl two stitches. Insert the left-hand needle into the back of the first stitch worked on the right-hand needle and lift this stitch over the second stitch and off the right-hand needle.

2 One stitch is now on the right-hand needle. Purl the next stitch. Repeat the first step until all the stitches have been cast off. Pull the yarn through the last stitch to fasten off.

decrease

knit 2 together

knit 2 together ('k2tog' or 'dec one')
On a knit row, insert the right-hand
needle from left to right through the
next two stitches on the left-hand needle
and knit them together. One stitch has
been decreased.

purl 2 together

purl 2 together ('p2tog' or 'dec one')
On a purl row, insert the right-hand
needle from right to left through the
next two stitches on the left-hand
needle. Then purl them together.
One stitch has been decreased.

slip stitch over

Decreases are used to make the
fabric narrower by getting rid of
stitches on the needle. They are
worked to make an opening for
a neckline or shaping a sleeve
head. As with increases they
can be used to create decorative
detail, often around a neck edge.
Increases and decreases are used
together to create lace patterns.

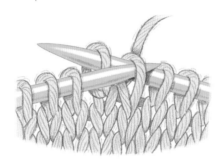

**slip 1, knit 1, pass slipped stitch
over ('psso')**
1 Insert the right-hand needle into
the next stitch on the left-hand needle
and slip it onto the right-hand needle
without knitting it. Knit the next stitch.
Then insert the left-hand needle into
the slipped stitch as shown.

2 With the left-hand needle, lift the
slipped stitch over the knitted stitch as
shown and off the right-hand needle.

reading patterns

To those unfamiliar with knitting patterns they can appear to be written in a strange, alien language! However as you become used to the terminology you will see that they have a logic and consistency that you will soon become familiar with.

Do not be too concerned if you read through a pattern first and are confused by parts of it as some instructions make more sense when your stitches are on the needle and you are at that point in the piece. However, it is sometimes a good idea to check with your retailer whether your skill levels are up to a particular design as this can prevent frustration later on.

Figures for larger sizes are given in round ( ) brackets. Where only one figure appears it means that those numbers apply to all sizes. Figures in square brackets [ ] are to be worked the number of times stated after the brackets. Where 0 appears, no stitches or rows are worked for this size.

When you follow the pattern it is important that you consistently use the right stitches or rows for your size, and you don't switch inside the brackets. This can be avoided by marking off your size throughout with a highlighting pen, but photocopy the pattern first so that you don't spoil your book.

Before starting your project, check the size and the actual measurements that are quoted for that size; you may want to make a smaller or larger garment depending on the proportions of the wearer it is intended for.

The quantities of yarn quoted in the instructions are based on the yarn used by the knitter of the original garment and therefore all amounts should be considered approximate. For example, if that knitter has used almost all of the last ball it may be that another knitter with a slightly different tension has to break into another ball to complete the garment. A slight variation in tension can therefore make the difference between using fewer or more balls than that stated in the pattern.

tension

Every knitting pattern will state a tension or gauge – the number of stitches and rows to 10cm that should be obtained with the quoted yarn, needle size and stitch pattern. It is vital to check your tension before starting your project. A slight variation can alter the proportions of the finished garment and the look of the fabric. A too loose tension will produce an uneven and unstable fabric that can drop or lose its shape after washing, whilst a too tight tension can make a hard, inelastic fabric.

Making a tension square

Use the same needles, yarn and stitch pattern quoted in the tension note in the pattern. Knit a sample at least 13cm square to get the most accurate result. Smooth out the finished sample on a flat surface making sure you are not stretching it out.

To check the stitch tension, place a tape measure or ruler horizontally on the sample and mark 10cm with pins. Count the number of stitches between the pins. To check the row tension, mark 10cm with pins vertically as before and count the number of rows. If the number of stitches and rows is greater than that quoted in the pattern, your tension is tighter and you should try changing to a larger needle and trying another tension square. If there are fewer stitches and rows, your tension is looser and you should try again on a smaller needle. The stitch tension is the most important to get right as the number of stitches in a pattern are set but the length is often calculated in measurement rather than rows and you may be able to work more or fewer rows.

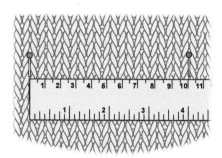

abbreviations

In a pattern book general abbreviations will usually be given at the front before the patterns begin, whilst those more specific to a particular design will be given at the start of the individual pattern. The following are the ones used throughout this book.

standard abbreviations

alt = alternate
beg = begin(ning)
cont = continue
dec = decrease (ing)
foll = following
inc = increase (ing)
k = knit
m1 = make one stitch by picking up the loop lying between the stitch just worked and the next stitch and working into the back of it
patt = pattern
p = purl
psso = pass slipped stitch over
rem = remain (ing)
rep = repeat (ing)
skpo = slip 1, knit 1, pass slipped stitch over
sl = slip
ssk = (slip 1 knitwise) twice, insert tip of left hand needle from left to right through slipped stitch and knit together
st(s) = stitch(es)
st st = stocking stitch
tbl = through back of loop
tog = together
yf = yarn forward
yon = yarn over needle
yrn = yarn round needle

stitch types

Once you have mastered the knit and purl stitches, you can combine the two to create an endless variety of stitch patterns. Each stitch pattern has its own character, and most knitters have a particular favourite. Mine is moss stitch, which I use in many of my designs.

garter stitch

Garter stitch is made of all knit rows, which create a dense, reversible fabric. It is particularly good for plain garments without borders as the fabric lies flat and doesn't curl up at the edges. Garter stitch gives new knitters the opportunity to create simple garments without welts or borders.

Cast on any number of stitches.
Knit every row.
Repeat this row to form garter stitch.

stocking stitch

Stocking stitch, the most commonly used pattern, is worked using alternate knit and purl rows. The purl row is considered to be the wrong side, but you can make either side the right or wrong side depending on the effect you want. The purl side of stocking stitch when used as the right side is called reverse stocking stitch.

Cast on any number of stitches.
1st row (right side) Knit.
2nd row (wrong side) Purl.

Repeat the first and second rows to form stocking stitch.

single rib or 1 x 1 rib

Ribbing is made by alternating vertical columns of knit and purl stitches. The knitter changes from knit to purl within the row rather than every other row. Ribbing can be used as an allover pattern, but it's elasticity makes it perfect for borders such as neckbands and cuffs as it stretches and springs back into shape to fit the body.

Cast on an even number of stitches.
1st row *K1, p1, repeat from * to end.
Repeat this row to form single rib.

double rib or 2 x 2 rib

Cast on a multiple of 4 stitches, plus 2.
1st row K2,*p2, k2, repeat from * to end.
2nd row P2,*k2, p2, repeat from * to end.
Repeat the first and second rows to form double rib.

moss stitch

Moss stitch is one of the most attractive of the simple stitch patterns. The reversible fabric is achieved by working knit and purl stitches that alternate vertically and horizontally. It works well as a stand-alone pattern but is also a good alternative to rib to provide decorative detail.

Cast on an uneven number of stitches.
1st row K1,*p1, k1, repeat from * to end.
Repeat this row to form moss stitch.

moss stitch

stocking stitch

garter stitch

double rib

single rib

cables

back cross cable

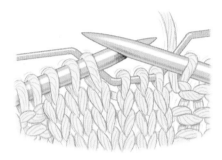

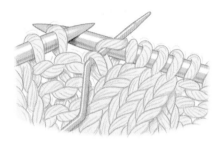

1 Slip the first three cable stitches purlwise off the left-hand needle and onto the cable needle. Leave the cable needle at the back of the work, then knit the next three stitches on the left-hand needle, keeping the yarn tight to prevent a gap from forming in the knitting.

2 Knit the three stitches directly from the cable needle, or if preferred, slip the three stitches from the cable needle back onto the left-hand needle and then knit them. This completes the cable cross.

front cross cable

Cables are formed by the simple technique of crossing one set of stitches over another. Stitches are held on a cable needle (a short double-pointed needle) at the back or front of the work while the same amount of stitches is worked from the left-hand needle. Simple cables form a vertical twisted rope of stocking stitch on a background of reverse stocking stitch and tend to be worked over four or six stitches.

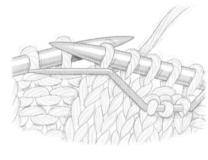

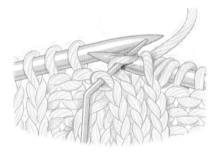

1 Slip the first three cable stitches purlwise off the left-hand needle and onto the cable needle. Leave the cable needle at the front of the work, then knit the next three stitches on the left-hand needle, keeping the yarn tight to prevent a gap from forming in the knitting.

2 Knit the three stitches directly from the cable needle, or if preferred, slip the three stitches from the cable needle back onto the left-hand needle and then knit them. This completes the cable cross.

intarsia

Intarsia is used when you are working with larger areas of usually isolated colour, such as when knitting motifs. If the yarn not in use was stranded or woven behind, it could show through to the front or pull in the colour work. In intarsia you use separate strands or small balls of yarn for each colour area and then twist them together where they meet to prevent a gap forming.

vertical

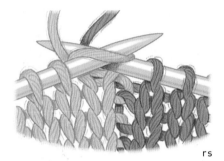

rs

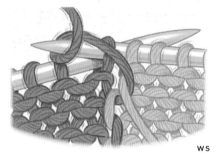

ws

right diagonal

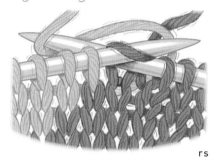

rs

ws

left diagonal

rs

ws

changing colours on a vertical line
If the two colour areas are forming a vertical line, to change colours on a knit row drop the colour you were using. Pick up the new colour and wrap it around the dropped colour as shown, then continue with the new colour. Twist the yarns together on knit and purl rows in this same way at vertical-line colour changes.

changing colours on a right diagonal
If the two colour areas are forming a right diagonal line, on a knit row drop the colour you were using. Pick up the new colour and wrap it around the dropped colour as shown, then continue with the new colour. Twist the yarns together on knit rows only at right-diagonal colour changes.

changing colours on a left diagonal
If the two colour areas are forming a left diagonal line, on a purl row drop the colour you were using. Pick up the new colour and wrap it around the colour just dropped as shown, then continue with the new colour. Twist the yarns together on purl rows only at left-diagonal colour changes.

reading charts

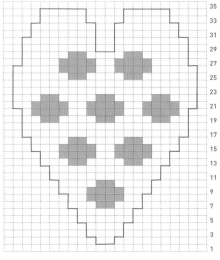

☐ A ecru ▨ C lime

Most colour patterns are worked from a chart rather than set out in the text. Each square represents a stitch and row and the symbol or colour within it will tell you which colour to use. There will be a key listing the symbols used and the colours they represent.

Unless stated otherwise, the first row of the chart is worked from right to left and represents the first right-side row of your knitting. The second chart row represents the second and wrong-side row and is read and worked from left to right.

If the colour pattern is a repeated design, as in Fair Isle, the chart will tell you how many stitches are in each repeat. You will repeat these stitches

as many times as is required. At each side of the repeat there may be edge stitches, these are only worked at the beginning and end of the rows and they indicate where you need to start and end for the piece you are knitting. Most colour patterns are worked in stocking stitch.

stranding

stranding on a knit row

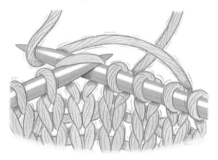

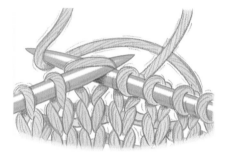

1 On a right-side (knit) row, to change colours drop the colour you were using. Pick up the new colour, take it over the top of the dropped colour and start knitting with it.

2 To change back to the old colour, drop the colour you were knitting with. Pick up the old colour, take it under the dropped colour and knit to the next colour change, and so on.

stranding on a purl row

Stranding is used when colour is worked over a small amount of stitches where using two colours in a row. The colour you are not using is left hanging on the wrong side of the work and then picked up when it is needed again. This creates strands at the back of the work called floats. Care must be taken so that they are not pulled too tightly as this will pucker the fabric. By picking up the yarns over and under one another you will prevent them tangling.

1 On a wrong-side (purl) row, to change colours drop the colour you were using. Pick up the new colour, take it over the top of the dropped colour and start purling with it.

2 To change back to the old colour, drop the colour you were knitting with. Pick up the old colour, take it under the dropped colour and purl to the next colour change, and so on.

&weaving in

weaving in on a knit row

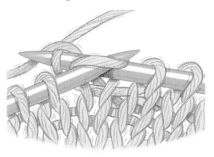 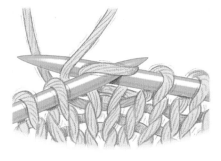

1 To weave in yarn on a knit stitch, insert the right-hand needle into the next stitch and lay the yarn to be woven in over the right-hand needle. Knit the stitch with the working yarn, taking it under the yarn not in use and making sure you do not catch this strand into the knitted stitch.

2 Knit the next stitch with the working yarn, taking it over the yarn being woven in. Continue like this, weaving the loose colour over and under the working yarn until you need to use it again.

weaving in on a purl row

When there are more than four stitches between a colour change, the floats are too long and this makes the fabric inflexible. The long strands can also catch when wearing the garment, particularly on the inside of a sleeve. By weaving in, the yarn not in use is caught up before the next colour change, thus shortening the float. Sometimes, depending on the colour pattern, a combination of both stranding and weaving can be used.

 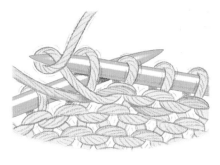

1 To weave in yarn on a purl stitch, insert the right-hand needle into the next stitch and lay the yarn to be woven in over the right-hand needle. Purl the stitch with the working yarn, taking it under the yarn not in use and making sure you do not catch this strand into the purled stitch.

2 Purl the next stitch with the working yarn, taking it over the yarn being woven in. Continue like this, weaving the loose colour over and under the working yarn until you need to use it again.

seaming

When you have completed the pieces of your knitting you reach one of the most important stages. The way you sew up or finish your project determines how good your finished garment will look. There are different types of seaming techniques but the best by far is mattress or ladder stitch, which creates an invisible seam. It can be used on stocking stitch, rib, garter and moss stitch.

The seam that I use for almost all sewing up is mattress stitch, which produces a wonderful invisible seam. It works well on any yarn, and makes a completely straight seam, as the same amount is taken up on each side – this also means that the knitted pieces should not need to be pinned together first. It is always worked on the right side of the fabric and is particularly useful for sewing up stripes and Fair Isle.

I use other types of seams less frequently, but they do have their uses. For instance, backstitch can sometimes be useful for sewing in a sleeve head, to neatly ease in the fullness. It is also good for catching in loose strands of yarn on colourwork seams, where there can be a lot of short ends along the selvedge. Just remember when using backstitch to sew up your knitting that it is important to ensure that you work in a completely straight line.

The seam for joining two cast-off edges is handy for shoulder seams, while the seam for joining a cast-off edge with a side edge (selvedge) is usually used when sewing a sleeve onto the body on a dropped shoulder style.

It is best to leave a long tail at the casting-on stage to sew up your knitting with, so that the sewing up yarn is already secured in place. If this is not possible, when first securing the thread for the seam, you should leave a length that can be darned in afterwards. All seams on knitting should be sewn with a large blunt-tipped yarn or tapestry needle to avoid splitting the yarn.

Before sewing up side seams, join the shoulder seams and attach the sleeves, unless they are set in sleeves. If there are any embellishments, such as applied pockets or embroidery, this is the time to put them on, when you can lay the garment out flat.

seams

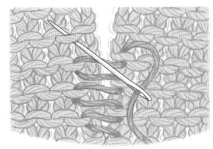

mattress stitch on stocking stitch and double rib
With the right sides of the knitting facing you, insert the needle under the horizontal bar between the first stitch and next stitch. Then insert the needle under the same bar on the other piece. Continue to do this, drawing up the thread to form the seam.

mattress stitch on garter stitch
With the right sides of the knitting facing you, insert the needle through the bottom of the 'knot' on the edge and then through the top of the corresponding 'knot' on the opposite edge. Continue to do this from edge to edge, drawing up the thread to form a flat seam.

mattress stitch on moss stitch
With the right sides of the knitting facing you, insert the needle under the horizontal bar between the first and second stitches on one side and through the top of the 'knot' on the edge of the opposite side.

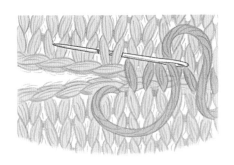

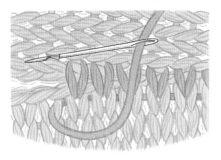

joining two cast-off edges (grafting)
1 With the cast-off edges butted together, bring the needle out in the centre of the first stitch just below the cast-off edge on one piece. Insert the needle through the centre of the first stitch on the other piece and out through the centre of the next stitch.

2 Next, insert the needle through the centre of the first stitch on the first piece again and out through the centre of the stitch next to it. Continue in this way until the seam is completed.

joining cast-off and selvedge edges
Bring the needle from back to front through the centre of the first stitch on the cast-off edge. Then insert it under one or two horizontal strands between the first and second stitches on the selvedge and back through the centre of the same cast-off stitch. Continue in this way until the seam is completed.

picking up stitches

When you are adding a border to your garment, such as front bands or a neckband, you usually pick up stitches around the edge. A border can be sewn on afterwards but this method is far neater. If you are picking up stitches along a long edge, a front band of a jacket for example, a long circular needle can be used so that you can fit all the stitches on. The pattern will usually tell you how many stitches to pick up.

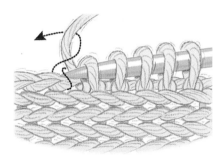

picking up stitches along a selvedge
With the right side of the knitting facing, insert the knitting needle from front to back between the first and second stitches of the first row. Wrap the yarn around the needle and pull a loop through to a form a new stitch on the needle. Continue in this way along the edge of the knitting.

picking up stitches along a neck edge
On a neck edge, work along the straight edges as for a selvedge. But along the curved edges, insert the needle through the centre of the stitch below the shaping (to avoid large gaps) and pull a loop of yarn through to form a new stitch on the needle.

knitting in the round

41

knitting in the round using a set of four needles

Working in the round is used for tubular, or seamless knitting. Stitches are divided evenly over three needles, with an extra needle used to knit the stitches. The needles form a triangle by drawing up the last cast-on stitch to meet the first cast-on. (Care should be taken to make sure that the cast-on edge is not twisted.) The fourth needle is used to knit the stitches from the first needle, and then as each needle becomes free, it is used to work the stitches from the next needle. When changing over from one needle to another, pull the yarn firmly to prevent a ladder forming. Keep track of the beginning of the round with a marker.

embroidery

Embroidery is a great way to enhance a simple jacket such as the Daisy Cardigan or to create a particular effect as in the Baby Blanket. For those who may be unsure of their skill with Fair Isle or intarsia, embroidery is a good way to add colour to a garment.

blanket stitch

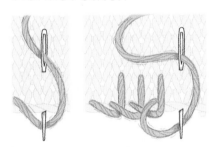

french knots

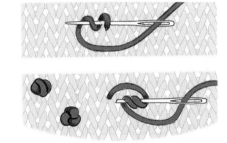

couching

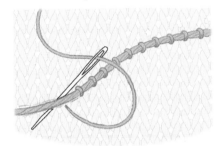

Although blanket stitch is usually used on the edge of a piece of knitting, the principle is the same for the eyelet detail on the Daisy Cardigan (see page 148). Secure the yarn to the edge of the fabric. After deciding on the height of the stitches you require and also the distance apart, insert the needle from front to back taking these requirements into account and making sure the yarn is under the needle tip at the edge of the fabric. Pull the yarn through, then re-insert the needle a short distance away, with the yarn once again under the needle. Repeat this until you have worked around the eyelet or along the edge and fasten off, making sure the last stitch is secure.

Bring the needle up and through the fabric. Wrap the yarn twice around it, holding the thread tautly. Re-insert the needle back through the fabric as close as possible to where it emerged, pulling the yarn to hold the wraps tight.

Place the yarn on the fabric following the outline. Using matching thread to 'couch', bring this thread through the fabric and over the yarn, then re-insert the needle as close as possible to where it emerged. Repeat along the length of the yarn to hold it in place. The more couching stitches you make, the more secure the yarn line will be.

pompons

Pompons are easy to create and good for decorative details on hats, scarves and cords. Children love to make them and they are a great way to introduce them to yarn before they learn to knit. For safety reasons, make sure that the pompon is tightly bound so that it cannot pull apart or disintegrate.

1 Cut two identical circles of cardboard which are slightly smaller than the size of the pompon you need. Cut a hole in the centre of each one and hold the circles together. Thread a darning needle with yarn and wind it continually through the centre and outer edges until the hole has closed.

2 Insert the tips of the scissors between the two circles and cut between and around the circles.

3 Tie a piece of yarn tightly between the two circles, and remove the cardboard.

patterns

classic cardigan

measurements

To fit ages 0–3 (3–6: 6–9: 9–12) months

finished measurements

Chest 42 (46: 50: 54) cm
Length to shoulder 20 (22: 25: 28) cm
Sleeve length 12 (14: 16: 18) cm

materials

3 (3: 3: 4) x 50g balls Debbie Bliss Baby Cashmerino in flax
Pair each 3mm and 3.25mm knitting needles
5 small buttons

tension

25 sts and 34 rows to 10cm square over st st using 3.25mm needles.

abbreviations

See page 25.

back

With 3mm needles, cast on 54 (58: 62: 66) sts.
1st rib row (right side) K2, * p2, k2; rep from * to end.
2nd rib row P2, * k2, p2; rep from * to end.
Rep the last 2 rows twice more, inc 1 (2: 3: 4) sts evenly across last row. **55 (60: 65: 70) sts.**
Change to 3.25mm needles.
Beg with a k row, work in st st until back measures 10 (11: 13: 15) cm from cast-on edge, ending with a p row.
Shape underarm
Cast off 4 sts at beg of next 2 rows. **47 (52: 57: 62) sts.**
Leave these sts on a spare needle.

left front

With 3mm needles, cast on 27 (27: 31: 35) sts.
1st rib row (right side) K2, * p2, k2; rep from * to last 5 sts, p2, k3.
2nd rib row P3, * k2, p2; rep from * to end.
Rep the last 2 rows twice more, inc 1 (3: 2: 0) sts evenly across last row. **28 (30: 33: 35) sts.**
Change to 3.25mm needles.
Beg with a k row, work in st st until front measures 10 (11: 13: 15) cm from cast-on edge, ending with a p row.
Shape underarm
Cast off 4 sts at beg of next row. **24 (26: 29: 31) sts.**
Leave these sts on a spare needle.

right front

With 3mm needles, cast on 27 (27: 31: 35) sts.
1st rib row (right side) K3, * p2, k2; rep from * to end.

2nd rib row P2, * k2, p2; rep from * to last 5 sts, k2, p3.
Rep the last 2 rows twice more, inc 1 (3: 2: 0) sts evenly across last row. 28 (30: 33: 35) sts.
Change to 3.25mm needles.
Beg with a k row, work in st st until front measures 10 (11: 13: 15) cm from cast-on edge, ending with a k row.

Shape underarm
Cast off 4 sts at beg of next row. 24 (26: 29: 31) sts.
P 1 row,
Leave these sts on a spare needle.

sleeves

With 3mm needles, cast on 34 (38: 38: 42) sts.
1st rib row K2, * p2, k2; rep from * to end.
2nd rib row P2, * k2, p2; rep from * to end.
Rep the last 2 rows twice more, inc 3 (0: 3: 2) sts evenly across last row. 37 (38: 41: 44) sts.
Change to 3.25mm needles.
Beg with a k row, work in st st.
Work 4 rows.
Inc row K3, m1, k to last 3 sts, m1, k3.
Work 5 rows.
Rep the last 6 rows until there are 45 (50: 55: 60) sts.

Cont straight until sleeve measures 12 (14: 16: 18) cm from cast-on edge, ending with a p row.

Shape underarm

Cast off 4 sts at beg of next 2 rows. **37 (42: 47: 52) sts.**

Leave these sts on a spare needle.

yoke

With right side facing and 3.25mm needles, k across 24 (26: 29: 31) sts from right front, 37 (42: 47: 52) sts from right sleeve, 47 (52: 57: 62) sts from back, 37 (42: 47: 52) sts from left sleeve, 24 (26: 29: 31) sts from left front. **169 (188: 209: 228) sts.**

Next row (wrong side) P to end.

Next row K21 (23: 26: 28), k2tog, k2, skpo, k31 (36: 41: 46), k2tog, k2, skpo, k41 (46: 51: 56), k2tog, k2, skpo, k31 (36: 41: 46), k2tog, k2, skpo, k21 (23: 26: 28).

Work 3 rows.

Next row K20 (22: 25: 27), k2tog, k2, skpo, k29 (34: 39: 44), k2tog, k2, skpo, k39 (44: 49: 54), k2tog, k2, skpo, k29 (34: 39: 44), k2tog, k2, skpo, k20 (22: 25: 27).

Next row P to end.

Next row K19 (21: 24: 26), k2tog, k2, skpo, k27 (32: 37: 42), k2tog, k2, skpo, k37 (42: 47: 52), k2tog, k2, skpo, k27 (32: 37: 42), k2tog, k2, skpo, k19 (21: 24: 26).

Next row P to end.

Next row K18 (20: 23: 25), k2tog, k2, skpo, k25 (30: 35: 40), k2tog, k2, skpo, k35 (40: 45: 50), k2tog, k2, skpo, k25 (30: 35: 40), k2tog, k2, skpo, k18 (20: 23: 25).

Next row P to end.

Cont in this way decreasing 8 sts on every right-side row until 65 (68: 73: 76) sts rem, ending with a k row.

Next row P to end, decreasing 1 (0: 1: 0) st at centre back. **64 (68: 72: 76) sts.**

Change to 3mm needles.

1st rib row (right side) K3, * p2, k2; rep from * to last 5 sts, p2, k3.

2nd rib row P3, * k2, p2; rep from * to last 5 sts, k2, p3.

Rep the last 2 rows twice more.

Cast off in rib.

button band

With right side facing and 3mm needles, pick up and k58 (62: 70: 78) sts evenly along left front edge.

1st rib row P2, * k2, p2; rep from * to end.

2nd rib row K2, * p2, k2; rep from * to end.

Rep the last 2 rows once more and the first row again.

Cast off in rib.

buttonhole band

With right side facing and 3mm needles, pick up and k58 (62: 70: 78) sts evenly along right front edge.

1st rib row (wrong side) P2, * k2, p2; rep from * to end.

2nd rib row K2, * p2, k2; rep from * to end.

Buttonhole row (wrong side) Rib 2, [rib 2tog, yrn, rib 11 (12: 14: 16)] 4 times, k2tog, yrn, p2.

Rib 2 more rows.

Cast off in rib.

to make up

Join side and sleeve seams. Join underarm seams. Sew on buttons.

size
Approximately 45 x 71cm

materials
1 x 50g ball Debbie Bliss Baby Cashmerino in grey (A)
2 x 50g balls Debbie Bliss Baby Cashmerino in each of pale peach (B), silver (C) and ecru (D)
Pair 3.25mm knitting needles
3.25mm circular knitting needle

tension
25 sts and 50 rows to 10cm square over garter st using 3.25mm needles.

abbreviations
See page 25.

striped blanket

note
When working the stripe pattern in B, C and D, do not break off yarn but carry the colours not in use up the side edge, making sure not to pull too tightly or the blanket will be distorted.

to make

With 3.25mm needles and A, cast on 107 sts.
K 4 rows.
Break off yarn.
Cont in garter st and work in stripe sequence as follows: 2 rows C, 2 rows B, 2 rows D.
The last 6 rows form the striped pattern and are repeated throughout.
Cont in pattern until work measures 70cm from cast-on edge.
Change to A and k 4 rows.
Cast off.

side edgings

With 3.25mm circular needle and A, pick up and k117 sts along one side edge of blanket and k 4 rows.
Cast off.
Repeat on other side edge.

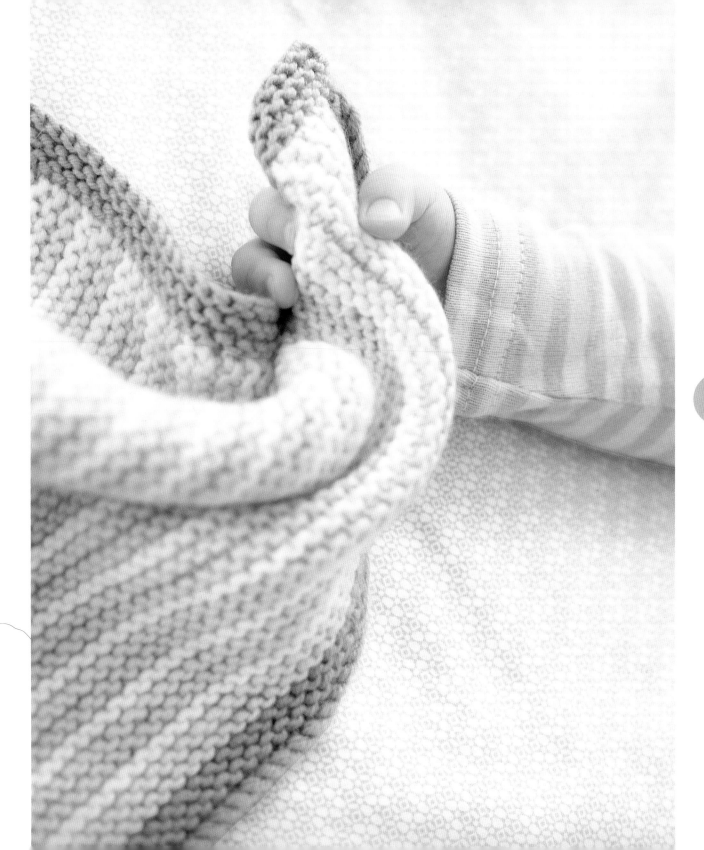

striped mouse

size
Approximately 18cm high

materials
Mouse 1 x 50g ball Debbie Bliss Baby Cashmerino in grey (A) and oddments of pale peach (B)
Pair 2.75mm knitting needles
Oddments of embroidery thread for eyes, snout and whiskers
Washable toy stuffing (see Note on opposite page)
Dress Oddments of Debbie Bliss Baby Cashmerino in grey (A), pale peach (B), silver (C) and ecru (D)
Pair 3.25mm knitting needles
Small button

tension
25 sts and 40 rows to 10cm square over st st using 2.75mm needles.

abbreviations
kfbf = knit into front, back and front of next st.
s2togkpo = slip 2 sts tog, k1, pass 2 slipped sts over.

note

Make sure you use a washable toy stuffing that is also non-flammable (flame retardant) and non-toxic and adheres to UK and EU safety regulations (BS5852, BS1425, EN71, PT2).

body

With 2.75mm needles and A, cast on 9 sts and p 1 row.
Next row (right side) [Kfb] 4 times, kfbf, [kfb] 4 times. **19 sts.**
P 1 row.
Next row K5, m1, k1, m1, k8, m1, k1, m1, k4. **23 sts.**
P 1 row.
Next row K6, m1, k1, m1, [k5, m1] twice, k1, m1, k5. **28 sts.**
P 1 row.
Next row K14, m1, k1, m1, k13. **30 sts.**
Beg with a p row, work 17 rows in st st.
Next row K5, k2tog, k1, ssk, k3, ssk, k1, k2tog, k3, k2tog, k1, ssk, k4. **24 sts.**
P 1 row.
Next row K4, k2tog, k1, ssk, k2, ssk, k3, k2tog, k1, ssk, k3. **19 sts.**
P 1 row.
Next row K3, k2tog, k1, ssk, k4, k2tog, k1, ssk, k2. **15 sts.**
P 1 row.
Next row K2, k2tog, k1, ssk, k2, k2tog, k1, ssk, k1. **11 sts.**
P 1 row.
Cast off.
Run a thread around the cast-off edge, pull up and join back seam, leaving a gap.
Stuff and close gap in seam.

head

With 2.75mm needles and A, cast on 4 sts and p 1 row.
Next row [Kfb] 3 times, k1. **7 sts.**
P 1 row.
Next row K1, [m1, k2, m1, k1] to end. **11 sts.**
Beg with a p row, work 3 rows in st st.
Next row K1, [m1, k3] 3 times, m1, k1.
P 1 row.
Next row K1, m1, k to last st, m1, k1.
Next row P1, m1, p to last st, m1, p1.
Next row K1, [m1, k3] twice, m1, k5, [m1, k3] twice, m1, k1. **25 sts.**
Place markers at each end of last row.
Beg with a p row, work 6 rows.
Next row P4, p2tog, p13, p2tog tbl, p4.
Next row K14, ssk, turn.
Next row Sl 1, p5, p2tog, turn.
Next row Sl 1, k5, ssk, turn.
Rep last 2 rows 6 times more.
Cast off purlwise, working last 2 sts tog.
Join seam from point of snout to markers, and stuff head.

outer ears (make 2)

With 2.75mm needles and A, cast on 7 sts.
Beg with a k row, work 4 rows in st st.
Next row Ssk, k3, k2tog.
P 1 row.
Next row Ssk, k1, k2tog.
Next row P3tog and fasten off.

inner ears (make 2)

With 2.75mm needles and B, cast on 6 sts.
Beg with a k row, work 3 rows in st st.
Next row P2tog, p2, p2tog tbl.
Next row Ssk, k2tog.
Next row P3tog and fasten off.

arms (make 2)

With 2.75mm needles and A, cast on 4 sts and p 1 row.
Next row [Kfb] 3 times, k1. **7 sts.**
P 1 row.
Next row [K1, m1, k2, m1] twice, k1. **11 sts.**
Beg with a p row, work 3 rows in st st.
Next row K3, ssk, k1, k2tog, k3. **9 sts.**
Beg with a p row, work 13 rows in st st.
Place markers at each end of last row.
Next row K1, ssk, k3, k2tog, k1. **7 sts.**
P 1 row.
Next row K1, ssk, k1, k2tog, k1. **5 sts.**
P 1 row.
Next row K1, s2togkpo, k1. **3 sts.**
P 1 row.
Next row S2togkpo. **1 st.**
Fasten off.
Join arm seam, from cast-on edge to markers, and stuff.

legs (make 2)

With 2.75mm needles and A, cast on 8 sts and p 1 row.
Next row (right side) [Kfb] 7 times, k1. **15 sts.**
P 1 row.
Next row K1, m1, k4, [m1, k1] 6 times, k3, m1, k1. **23 sts.**
Beg with a p row, work 3 rows in st st.
Next row K9, k2tog, k1, ssk, k9. **21 sts.**
P 1 row.
Next row K8, k2tog, k1, ssk, k8. **19 sts.**
Next row P7, p2tog tbl, p1, p2tog, p7. **17 sts.**
Next row K7, s2togkpo, k7. **15 sts.**
P 1 row.
Next row K5, ssk, k1, k2tog, k5. **13 sts.**
Beg with a p row, work 23 rows in st st.

Next row K1, [ssk] twice, k3, [k2tog] twice, k1. **9 sts.**
P 1 row.
Next row K1, ssk, k3, k2tog, k1. **7 sts.**
Next row P1, p2tog, p1, p2tog tbl, p1.
Break yarn, thread through rem 5 sts, pull up and secure.
Join leg seam, leaving a gap for stuffing. Stuff foot and leg, then close gap in seam.

tail

With 2.75mm needles and A, cast on 25 sts.
Cast off.

to finish

Sew ears together in pairs of inner and outer ear pieces and sew to head. Using embroidery thread, work eyes, snout and whiskers. Sew head onto body, gathering slightly around neck edge. Sew arms in place around open edge. Sew on legs and tail.

dress

With 3.25mm needles and A, cast on 48 sts.
K 1 row.
* Change to C and k 2 rows.
Change to B and k 2 rows.
Change to D and k 2 rows.
Rep from * 3 times more.
Change to C and work as follows:
Next row (right side) K10, [k2tog] 14 times, k10. **34 sts.**
Divide for front and back yokes
Next row (wrong side) K6 (for right back), cast off 4 sts (for armhole), with one st on needle after cast off, k next 13 sts (for front), cast off 4 sts (for armhole), k to end (for left back).
Change to B and work as follows:
On first set of 6 sts (left back), k 13 rows.
Cast off knitwise.
With right side facing, rejoin B to 14 sts of front, k 13 rows.
Cast off knitwise.
With right side facing, rejoin B to 6 sts of right back, k 13 rows.
Cast off knitwise and leave a long length of yarn.
With the length of yarn, make a small button loop on edge of right back.
Join back seam from cast-on edge to beg of yoke.
Sew button onto left back.

babyshrug

measurements

To fit ages 3–6 (6–9: 9–12: 12–18: 18–24) months
actual measurements
Chest 51 (55: 60: 64: 69)cm
Length to shoulder 24 (27: 29: 31: 33)cm
Sleeve length 13 (15: 17: 20: 22)cm

materials

2 (3: 3: 4: 4) x 50g balls Debbie Bliss Cashmerino Aran in pale pink
Long circular and pair 5mm knitting needles
Long circular and pair 4.50mm knitting needles

tension

18 sts and 24 rows to 10cm square over st st using 5mm needles.

abbreviations

See page 25.

back, front & sleeves

Work in one piece.
With 5mm needles, cast on 8 sts.
P 1 row.
Beg with a k row, work in st st.
Cast on 10 (11: 12: 13: 14) sts at beg of next 4 rows. **48 (52: 56: 60: 64) sts.**
Beg with a k row, work 20 (24: 26: 30: 32) rows in st st.
Change to 5mm circular needle.

Shape sleeves

Cast on 5 (6: 7: 8: 9) sts at beg of next 8 rows. **88 (100: 112: 124: 136) sts.**
Work a further 18 (22: 24: 26: 28) rows.

Divide for fronts

Next row K36 (41: 47: 52: 58) sts, leave these sts on a spare needle, cast off next 16 (18: 18: 20: 20) sts, k to end.
Cont on last set of 36 (41: 47: 52: 58) sts for left front.
Work 5 (5: 7: 5: 7) rows straight, ending at front edge.
Next row (right side) K3, m1, k to end.
Work 3 rows straight.
Rep the last 4 rows 2 (3: 3: 4: 4) times more and the inc row once more. **40 (46: 52: 58: 64) sts.**

Sleeve shaping

Cast off 5 (6: 7: 8: 9) sts at beg of next row and 3 foll alt rows. **20 (22: 24: 26: 28) sts.**
Work 8 (10: 10: 12: 12) rows straight.

Shape front

Next row (right side) K1, skpo, k to end.
Next row P to end.
Rep the last 2 rows 1 (2: 3: 4: 5) times more.
Next row Cast off 2 sts, k to end.
Next row P to end.
Next row Cast off 3 sts, k to end.
Next row P to end.
Next row Cast off 4 sts, k to end.
Next row P to end.
Next row Cast off 5 sts, k to end.
Next row P to end.
Leave rem 4 (5: 6: 7: 8) sts on a holder.

Right front

With wrong side facing, join yarn to rem 36 (41: 47: 52: 58) sts on spare needle, p to end.
Work 4 (4: 6: 4: 6) rows straight, ending at side edge.
Next row (right side) K to last 3 sts, m1, k3.
Work 3 rows straight.
Rep the last 4 rows 2 (3: 3: 4: 4) times more and the inc row once more. **40 (46: 52: 58: 64) sts.**
Work 1 row, so ending at sleeve edge.

Sleeve shaping

Cast off 5 (6: 7: 8: 9) sts at beg of next row and 3 foll alt rows. **20 (22: 24: 26: 28) sts.**

Work 7 (9: 9: 11: 11) rows straight.
Shape front
Next row (right side) K to last 3 sts, k2tog, k1.
Next row P to end.
Rep the last 2 rows 1 (2: 3: 4: 5) times more.
Next row K to end.
Next row Cast off 2 sts, p to end.
Next row K to end.
Next row Cast off 3 sts, p to end.
Next row K to end.
Next row Cast off 4 sts, p to end.
Next row K to end.
Next row Cast off 5 sts, p to end.
Leave rem 4 (5: 6: 7: 8) sts on a holder.

front edging

With right side of lower right front facing and 4.50mm circular needle, k4 (5: 6: 7: 8) sts from holder, pick up and k22 (24: 26: 28: 30) sts evenly round right front to top of shaping, 11 (11: 13: 13: 15) sts along straight edge, then 16 (18: 20: 22: 24) sts to shoulder, 24 (26: 28: 30: 32) sts from back neck, 16 (18: 20: 22: 24) sts down left front to beg of neck shaping, 11 (11: 13: 13: 15) sts along straight edge, and k22 (24: 26: 28: 30) sts evenly round shaped edge, then k4 (5: 6: 7: 8) sts from holder. **130 (142: 158: 170: 186) sts.**
1st row P2, * k2, p2; rep from * to end.
2nd row K2, * p2, k2; rep from * to end.
Rep the last 2 rows once more and 1st row again.
Cast off in rib.

lower back edging

With right side facing and 4.50mm needles, pick up and k54 (58: 62: 66: 70) sts along lower edge of back.
Work 5 rows in rib as given for front edging.
Cast off in rib.

cuffs

With right side facing and 4.50mm needles, pick up and k30 (34: 42: 46: 50) sts along lower edge of sleeve.
Work 5 rows in rib as given for front edging.
Cast off in rib.

to make up

Join side and sleeve seams.

duffel coat

measurements

To fit ages 0–3 (3–6: 6–9: 9–12) months

finished measurements

Chest 48 (52: 57: 61) cm

Length to shoulder 21 (24: 26: 28) cm

Sleeve length (with cuff turned back) 13 (15: 17: 19) cm

materials

6 (6: 7: 8) x 50g balls Debbie Bliss Rialto DK in grey

Pair each 3.25mm and 4mm knitting needles

4 buttons

tension

22 sts and 48 rows to 10cm square over garter st using 4mm needles.

abbreviations

See page 25.

back

With 4mm needles, cast on 53 (57: 63: 67) sts.
Work in garter st (k every row) until back measures 12 (14: 15: 16) cm from cast-on edge, ending with a wrong-side row.
Shape armholes
Cast off 4 sts at beg of next 2 rows. **45 (49: 55: 59) sts.**
Cont straight until back measures 21 (24: 26: 28) cm from cast-on edge, ending with a wrong-side row.
Shape shoulders
Cast off 11 (12: 14: 15) sts at beg of next 2 rows.
Cast off rem 23 (25: 27: 29) sts.

pocket linings
(make 2)

With 4mm needles, cast on 12 (13: 15: 16) sts.
K 28 (30: 32: 34) rows.
Leave these sts on a holder.

left front

With 4mm needles, cast on 38 (41: 45: 48) sts.
K 27 (29: 31: 33) rows.
Place pocket
Next row (right side) K3, cast off next 12 (13: 15: 16) sts, k to end.
Next row K23 (25: 27: 29), k across sts of first pocket lining, k3.
Cont in garter st until front measures 12 (14: 15: 16) cm from cast-on edge, ending with a wrong-side row.
Shape armhole
Cast off 4 sts at beg of next row. **34 (37: 41: 44) sts.**
Cont straight until front measures same as Back to shoulder, ending at armhole edge.
Shape shoulder
Next row Cast off 11 (12: 14: 15) sts, k to end.
K 1 row.
Leave rem 23 (25: 27: 29) sts on a spare needle.

right front

With 4mm needles, cast on 38 (41: 45: 48) sts.
K 27 (29: 31: 33) rows.
Place pocket
Next row K23 (25: 27: 29), cast off next 12 (13: 15: 16) sts, k to end.
Next row K3, k across sts of second pocket lining, k to end.
Cont in garter st until front measures 8 (9: 9: 9) cm from cast-on edge, ending with a wrong-side row.
Buttonhole row K3, yf, k2tog, k13 (15: 17: 19), k2tog, yf, k to end.
Cont in garter st until front measures 12 (14: 15: 16) cm from cast-on edge, ending with a right-side row.

Shape armhole

Cast off 4 sts at beg of next row. **34 (37: 41: 44) sts.**

Cont straight until front measures 13 (15: 16: 17)cm from cast-on edge, ending with a wrong-side row.

Buttonhole row K3, yf, k2tog, k13 (15: 17: 19), k2tog, yf, k to end.

Cont straight until front measures same as Back to shoulder, ending at armhole edge.

Shape shoulder

Next row Cast off 11 (12: 14: 15) sts, k to end. **23 (25: 27: 29) sts.**

Do not break yarn, leave sts on the needle.

hood

Join shoulder seams.

Next row (right side) K23 (25: 27: 29) sts from right front, cast on 34 (37: 40: 44) sts, k23 (25: 27: 29) sts from left front. **80 (87: 94: 102) sts.**

Cont in garter st until hood measures 18 (20: 22: 24)cm, ending with a wrong-side row.

Cast off.

sleeves

With 4mm needles, cast on 29 (31: 33: 35) sts.

K 13 (13: 17: 17) rows.

Change to 3.25mm needles.

K 12 (12: 16: 16) rows.

Change to 4mm needles.

Inc and work into garter st 1 st at each end of the next row and every foll 8th row until there are 41 (45: 49: 53) sts.

Cont straight until sleeve measures 17 (19: 22: 24)cm from cast-on edge, ending with a wrong-side row.

Mark each edge of last row with a coloured thread.

Work a further 8 rows.

Cast off.

to make up

Fold hood in half and join top seam. Easing in fullness, join cast-on edge of hood to sts cast off at back neck. Matching centre of cast-off edge of sleeve to shoulder, sew sleeves into armholes, with row ends above markers sewn to sts cast off at underarm. Join side and sleeve seams. Sew down pocket linings. Sew on buttons.

measurements

To fit ages 0–3 (3–6: 6–9: 9–12:) months
finished measurements
Chest 45 (50: 53: 58) cm
Length to shoulder 21 (24: 26: 28) cm

materials

2 (2: 3: 3) x 50g balls Debbie Bliss Baby Cashmerino in flax
Pair each 3mm and 3.25mm knitting needles
3mm circular knitting needle
One small button

tension

25 sts and 34 rows to 10cm square over st st using 3.25mm needles.

abbreviations

See page 25.

tank top

back

With 3.25mm needles, cast on 59 (65: 68: 74) sts.

1st row (right side) K2, * p1, k2; rep from * to end.

2nd row P.

Rep the last 2 rows twice more.

Now work in patt as follows:

1st row (right side) K2 (5: 2: 5), * p1, k8; rep from * to last 6 sts, p1, k2 (5: 2: 5).

2nd row P.

These 2 rows **form** the patt and are repeated.

Cont in patt until back measures 11 (13: 14: 15) cm from cast-on edge, ending with a p row.

Shape armholes

Cast off 3 (4: 4: 5) sts at beg of next 2 rows. 53 (57: 60: 64) sts.

Dec 1 st at each end of next row and 3 (3: 4: 4) foll alt rows. 45 (49: 50: 54) sts. **

Cont in patt until back measures 15 (17: 19: 22) cm from cast-on edge, ending with a wrong-side row.

Back neck opening

1st row (right side) Patt 22 (24: 25: 27) sts, turn and work on these sts only for first side of neck shaping, leaving rem sts on a spare needle.

2nd row Cast on 2 sts, then work k2, p to end. 24 (26: 27: 29) sts.

Next row Patt to last 2 sts, k2.

Next row K2, p to end.

Rep the last 2 rows until back measures 19 (22: 24: 26) cm from cast-on edge, ending with a wrong-side row.

Shape neck

Next row K15 (16: 17: 18) sts, turn, leaving rem 9 (10: 10: 11) sts on a safety pin.

Next row P1, p2tog, p to end.

Next row Patt to last 3 sts, k2tog, k1.

Rep the last 2 rows once more. 11 (12: 13: 14) sts.

Work 3 rows in patt.

Cast off for shoulder.

With right side facing, rejoin yarn to sts on spare needle, k2, patt to end.

Next row P to last 2 sts, k2.

Next row K2, patt to end.

Rep the last 2 rows until back measures 19 (22: 24: 26) cm from cast-on edge, ending with a right-side row.

Shape neck

Next row P12 (13: 14: 15) sts, p2tog tbl, p1, turn, leaving rem 8 (9: 8: 9) sts on a safety pin.

Next row K1, skpo, patt to end.

Next row P to last 3 sts, p2tog tbl, p1.

Next row K1, skpo, patt to end. 11 (12: 13: 14) sts.

Work 3 rows in patt.

Cast off for shoulder.

front

Work as given for Back to **.

Cont in patt until front measures 15 (18: 20: 22) cm from cast-on edge, ending with a wrong-side row.

Shape neck

Next row K18 (20: 20: 22) sts, turn and work on these sts only for first side of front neck, leaving rem sts on a spare needle.

Next row Cast off 2 sts, p to end.

Patt 1 row.

Rep the last 2 rows once more. **14 (16: 16: 18) sts.**

Next row P1, p2tog, p to end.

Patt 1 row.

Rep the last 2 rows 2 (3: 2: 3) times more. **11 (12: 13: 14) sts.**

Work straight until front measures same as Back to shoulder, ending with a p row.

Cast off for shoulder.

With right side facing, slip centre 9 (9: 10: 10) sts onto a holder, rejoin yarn to rem sts on spare needle, patt to end.

Next row P.

Next row Cast off 2 sts, patt to end.

Rep the last 2 rows once more. **14 (16: 16: 18) sts.**

Next row P to last 3 sts, p2tog tbl, p1.

Patt 1 row.

Rep the last 2 rows 2 (3: 2: 3) times more. **11 (12: 13: 14) sts.**

Work straight until front measures same as Back to shoulder, ending with a p row.

Cast off for shoulder.

neckband

Join shoulder seams.

With right side facing and 3 mm circular needle, slip 8 (9: 8: 9) sts from left back onto needle, pick up and k8 (8: 9: 9) sts up left back neck, 21 sts down left side of front neck, k across 9 (9: 10: 10) sts from front neck holder, pick up and k21 sts up right side of front neck, 8 sts down right back neck, then work p7 (8: 8: 9), k2 from back neck holder. **84 (86: 87: 89) sts.**

1st and 3rd sizes only

1st row (wrong side) K2, p1, * k1, p2; rep from * to last 3 sts, k3.

2nd row (buttonhole row) K1, yrn, p2tog, * k2, p1; rep from * to last 3 sts, k3.

3rd row K2, p1, * k1, p2; rep from * to last 3 sts, k3.

4th row K2, [p1, k2] 4 times, p1, [k2tog, p1, k2, p1] 4 times, k2tog, p1, k0 (-: 2: -), p0 (-: 1: -), k2tog, [p1, k2, p1, k2tog] 4 times, [p1, k2] 5 times, k1.

Cast off knitwise.

2nd and 4th sizes only

1st row (wrong side) K2, p2, * k1, p2; rep from * to last 4 sts, k1, p1, k2.

2nd row (buttonhole row) K1, yf, k2tog, * p1, k2; rep from * to last 2 sts, k2.

3rd row K2, p2, *k1, p2; rep from * to last 4 sts, k1, p1, k2.

4th row K3, [p1, k2] 4 times, [k2tog, p1, k2, p1] 4 times, k2tog, p1, k- (0: -: 2), p- (0: -: 1), k2tog, [p1, k2, p1, k2tog] 4 times, [p1, k2] 5 times, k2.

Cast off knitwise.

armbands

With right side facing and 3 mm needles, pick up and k65 (71: 77: 83) sts around armhole edge.

1st row (wrong side) P5, [k1, p2] to last 6 sts, k1, p5.

2nd row K5, * p1, k2; rep from * to last 6 sts, p1, k5.

3rd row As 1st row.

1st and 3rd sizes only

4th row K5, [p1, k2tog, p1, k2] 4 (-: 5: -) times, p1, [k2tog, p1] twice, [k2, p1, k2tog, p1] 4 (-: 5: -) times, k5. **55 (-: 65: -) sts.**

2nd and 4th sizes only

4th row K5, [p1, k2, p1, k2tog] – (5: -: 6) times, p1, [k2tog, p1, k2, p1] – (5: -: 6) times, k5. **– (61: -: 71) sts.**

All sizes

Cast off knitwise.

to make up

Join side and armband seams. Sew lower end of left back button band behind right back buttonhole band. Sew on button.

cablesweater (81)

measurements
To fit ages 3–6 (6–9: 9–12: 12–18: 18–24) months
actual measurements
Chest 50 (57: 61: 68: 73)cm
Length to shoulder 26 (28: 30: 33: 36)cm
Sleeve length 16 (18: 20: 22: 24)cm

materials
4 (4: 5: 5: 6) x 50g balls Debbie Bliss Baby Cashmerino in pale blue (M) and 1 x 50g ball in ecru (C)
Pair each 3mm and 3.25mm knitting needles
Cable needle

tension
25 sts and 34 rows to 10cm square over st st using 3.25mm needles.

abbreviations
C4F = slip next 2 sts onto cable needle and hold at front of work, k2, then k2 from cable needle.
m1p = make one st by picking up and purling into back of loop between st just worked and next st.
See page 25.

back

With 3mm needles and C, cast on 74 (82: 90: 98: 106) sts.
1st row (right side) K2, * p2, k2; rep from * to end.
2nd row P2, * k2, p2; rep from * to end.
Change to M.
Rib a further 4 rows.
Change to C.
Rib 2 rows.
Change to M.
Rib 1 row.
Inc row (wrong side) P2, k2 (0: 2: 0: 2), p2 (0: 2: 0: 2), * k2, m1p, p2, m1p, k2, p2; rep from * to last 4 (0: 4: 0: 4) sts, k2 (0: 2: 0: 2), p2 (0: 2: 0: 2). **90 (102: 110: 122: 130) sts.**
Change to 3.25mm needles.
Work in patt as follows:
1st row K2, p2 (0: 2: 0: 2), k2 (0: 2: 0: 2), * p2, k4, p2, k2; rep from * to last 4 (0: 4: 0: 4) sts, p2 (0: 2: 0: 2), k2 (0: 2: 0: 2).
2nd row P2, k2 (0: 2: 0: 2), p2 (0: 2: 0: 2), * k2, p4, k2, p2; rep from * to last 4 (0: 4: 0: 4) sts, k2 (0: 2: 0: 2), p2 (0: 2: 0: 2).
3rd row K2, p2 (0: 2: 0: 2), k2 (0: 2: 0: 2), * p2, C4F, p2, k2; rep from * to last 4 (0: 4: 0: 4) sts, p2 (0: 2: 0: 2), k2 (0: 2: 0: 2).
4th row As 2nd row.
5th row K2, p2 (0: 2: 0: 2), k2 (0: 2: 0: 2), * p2, k4, p2, k2; rep from * to last 4 (0: 4: 0: 4) sts, p2 (0: 2: 0: 2), k2 (0: 2: 0: 2).
6th row As 2nd row.
These 6 rows **form** the patt.
Cont in patt until back measures 15 (16: 17: 19: 21)cm from cast-on edge, ending with a wrong side row.
Shape armholes
Cast off 3 sts at beg of next 2 rows. **84 (96: 104: 116: 124) sts.****
Cont in patt until back measures 26 (28: 30: 33: 36)cm from cast-on edge, ending with a wrong side row.
Shape shoulders
Cast off 13 (15: 16: 18: 19) sts at beg of next 4 rows.
Leave rem 32 (36: 40: 44: 48) sts on a holder.

front

Work as given for Back to **.
Shape front neck
Next row (right side) Patt 39 (45: 49: 55: 59) sts, k2tog, turn and work on these sts for first side of front neck.
Next row Patt to end.
Next row Patt to last 2 sts, k2tog.
Rep the last 2 rows until 26 (30: 32: 36: 38) sts rem.
Cont straight until front measures same as Back to shoulder, ending at armhole edge.
Shape shoulder
Cast off 13 (15: 16: 18: 19) sts at beg of next row.
Work 1 row.
Cast off rem 13 (15: 16: 18: 19) sts.

With right side facing, slip centre 2 sts onto a safety pin, join yarn to rem sts, skpo, patt to end.
Next row Patt to end
Next row Skpo, patt to end.
Rep the last 2 rows until 26 (30: 32: 36: 38) sts rem.
Cont straight until front measures same as Back to shoulder, ending at armhole edge.
Shape shoulder
Cast off 13 (15: 16: 18: 19) sts at beg of next row.
Work 1 row.
Cast off rem 13 (15: 16: 18: 19) sts.

sleeves

With 3mm needles and C, cast on 34 (42: 42: 50: 50) sts.
1st row (right side) K2, * p2, k2; rep from * to end.
2nd row P2, * k2, p2; rep from * to end.
Change to M.
Rib a further 4 rows.
Change to C.
Rib 2 rows.
Change to M.
Rib 1 row.
Inc row (wrong side) P2, * k2, m1p, p2, m1p, k2, p2; rep from * to end. 42 (52: 52: 62: 62) sts.
Change to 3.25mm needles.
Work in patt as follows:
1st row (right side) K2, * p2, k4, p2, k2; rep from * to end.
2nd row P2, * k2, p4, k2, p2; rep from * to end.

3rd row K2, * p2, C4F, p2, k2; rep from * to end.

4th row As 2nd row.

5th row K2, * p2, k4, p2, k2; rep from * to end.

6th row As 2nd row.

These 6 rows **set** the patt.

Inc and work into patt 1 st at each end of the next (3rd: next: 5th: next) row and every foll
3rd (4th: 3rd: 3rd: 3rd) row until there are 62 (72: 82: 92: 102) sts.

Cont straight until sleeve measures 16 (18: 20: 22: 24)cm from cast-on edge, ending with a wrong
side row.

Mark each end of last row with a coloured thread.

Work a further 4 rows.

Cast off.

neckband

Join right shoulder seam.

With right side facing, 3mm needles and M, pick up and k40 (43: 45: 47: 49) sts evenly down left
side of front neck, k2 from safety pin, pick up and k38 (41: 43: 45: 47) sts evenly up right side of
front neck, k0 (0: 0: 0: 1), p0 (0: 0: 1: 2), k0 (0: 1: 2: 2), p0 (1: 2: 2: 2), k1 (0: 0: 0: 0), [k2tog]
1 (2: 2: 2: 2) times, p2, k2, p2, [k2tog] twice, p2, k2, p2, [k2tog] twice, p2, k2, p2, [k2tog] 1 (2: 2: 2: 2)
times, k1 (0: 0: 0: 0), p0 (1: 2: 2: 2), k0 (0: 1: 2: 2), p0 (0: 0: 1: 2), k0 (0: 0: 0: 1) across back neck sts.
106 (114: 122: 130: 138) sts.

Change to C.

1st size only

1st row P2, * k2, p2; rep from * to end.

2nd and 4th sizes only

1st row K1, * p2, k2; rep from * to last st, p1.

3rd and 5th sizes only

1st row P1,* k2, p2; rep from * to last st, k1.

All sizes

This row **sets** the rib patt.

2nd row Rib 39 (42: 44: 46: 48), k2tog, skpo, rib to end.

Change to M.

3rd row Rib to end.

4th row Rib 38 (41: 43: 45: 47), k2tog, skpo, rib to end

Change to C.

5th row Rib to end.

6th row Rib 37 (40: 42: 44: 46), k2tog, skpo, rib to end.

7th row Rib to end.

8th row Rib 36 (39: 41: 43: 45), k2tog, skpo, rib to end.

Change to M.

9th row Rib to end.

Cast off in rib, while decreasing as before.

to make up

Join left shoulder and neckband seam. Sew sleeves into armholes with row-ends above markers
sewn to sts cast off at underarm. Join side and sleeve seams.

cuff bootees

sizes
To fit ages 0–3 (3–6) months

materials
1 x 50g ball Debbie Bliss Baby Cashmerino in pale blue (M) and oddments in lime (C)
Pair each 2.75mm and 3mm knitting needles

tension
27 sts and 36 rows to 10cm square over st st using 3mm needles.

abbreviations
See page 25.

to make

With 2.75mm needles and M, cast on 26 sts.
1st row K to end.
2nd row K1, yf, k11, yf, k2, yf, k11, yf, k1.
3rd and every foll alt row K to end.
4th row K2, yf, k11, yf, k4, yf, k11, yf, k2.
6th row K3, yf, k11, yf, k6, yf, k11, yf, k3.
8th row K4, yf, k11, yf, k8, yf, k11, yf, k4.
10th row K5, yf, k11, yf, k10, yf, k11, yf, k5. **46 sts.**
12th row K6, yf, k11, yf, k12, yf, k11, yf, k6. **50 sts.**
13th row K to end.
2nd size only
14th row K7, yf, k11, yf, k14, yf, k11, yf, k7. **54 sts.**
15th row K to end.
Both sizes
Change to 3mm needles.

With C, k 2 rows.

Change to M.

Next row (right side) K to end.

Next row [K1, p1] 11 (12) times, k6, [p1, k1] 11 (12) times.

The last row forms the moss st with garter st instep and is repeated twice more.

Shape instep

Keeping moss st correct, work as follows:

1st row (right side) Moss st 21 (23), k2tog, k4, k2tog, moss st 21 (23).

2nd row Moss st 21 (23), k6, moss st 21 (23).

3rd row Moss st 20 (22), k2tog, k4, k2tog, moss st 20 (22).

4th row Moss st 20 (22), k6, moss st 20 (22).

5th row Moss st 19 (21), k2tog, k4, k2tog, moss st 19 (21).

6th row Moss st 19 (21), k6, moss st 19 (21).

Cont in this way to dec 2 sts on every right side row until 28 (30) sts rem, ending with a wrong side row.

Change to 2.75mm needles.

Work 10 rows straight.

Place a marker at each end of last row.

Change to 3mm needles.

Next row [K1, p1] 7 times, k0 (1), turn and work on these sts.

Work a further 10 rows in moss st.

Change to C.

K 2 rows.

Cast off.

With right side facing, 3mm needles and M, rejoin yarn to rem sts and work as follows:

Next row K0 (1), [p1, k1] 7 times.

Work a further 10 rows in moss st.

Change to C.

K 2 rows.

Cast off.

to make up   Join sole and back seam to markers, then reverse seam so allowing the cuff to fold onto right side.

hooded jacket

measurements

To fit ages 3–6 (6–9: 9–12: 12–18: 18–24) months
actual measurements
Chest 50 (54: 59: 63: 70)cm
Length to shoulder 27 (28: 32: 35: 39)cm
Sleeve length with rolled edge 14 (16: 18: 21: 23)cm

materials

4 (5: 6: 6: 7) x 50g balls Debbie Bliss Cashmerino Aran in apple green
Long circular and pair 5mm knitting needles
One large button

tension

18 sts and 24 rows to 10cm square over st st using 5mm needles.

abbreviations

y2rn = yarn twice round needle.
See page 25.

back

With 5mm needles, cast on 57 (61: 67: 73: 81) sts.
Beg with a k row, work in st st.
Work 6 rows.
Dec row K4, skpo, k to last 6 sts, k2tog, k4.
Work 5 rows.
Rep the last 6 rows 3 (3: 4: 5: 6) times more and the dec row again. **47 (51: 55: 59: 65) sts.**
Work straight until back measures 14 (15: 18: 20: 23)cm from cast-on edge, ending with a p row.
Shape armholes
Cast off 4 (4: 5: 5: 6) sts at beg of next 2 rows.
Leave the rem 39 (43: 45: 49: 53) sts on a spare needle.

left front

With 5mm needles, cast on 31 (33: 36: 39: 43) sts.
Next row K to end.
Next row K1, p to end.
These 2 rows set the st st with garter st edging.
Work 4 rows.
Dec row K4, skpo, k to end.
Work 5 rows.
Rep the last 6 rows 3 (3: 4: 5: 6) times more and the dec row again. **26 (28: 30: 32: 35) sts.**
Work straight until front measures 14 (15: 18: 20: 23)cm from cast-on edge, ending with a wrong side row.
Shape armhole
Cast off 4 (4: 5: 5: 6) sts at beg of next row.
Work 1 row.
Leave the rem 22 (24: 25: 27: 29) sts on a spare needle.

right front

With 5mm needles, cast on 31 (33: 36: 39: 43) sts.
Next row K to end.
Next row P to last st, k1.
These 2 rows set the st st with garter st edging.
Work 4 rows.
Dec row K to last 6 sts, k2tog, k4.
Work 5 rows.
Rep the last 6 rows 3 (3: 4: 5: 6) times more and the dec row again. **26 (28: 30: 32: 35) sts.**
Work straight until front measures 14 (15: 18: 20: 23)cm from cast-on edge, ending with a right side row.

Shape armhole
Cast off 4 (4: 5: 5: 6) sts at beg of next row.
Leave the rem 22 (24: 25: 27: 29) sts on a spare needle. Do not break off yarn.

sleeves

With 5mm needles, cast on 30 (32: 34: 36: 38) sts.
Beg with a k row, work in st st.
Work 8 (8: 8: 10: 10) rows.
Inc row K3, m1, k to last 3 sts, m1, k3.
Work 3 rows in st st.
Rep the last 4 rows 5 (6: 7: 8: 9) times more and the inc row again. **44 (48: 52: 56: 60) sts.**
Cont straight until sleeve measures 15 (17: 19: 22: 24)cm from cast-on edge, ending with a p row.

Shape top
Cast off 4 (4: 5: 5: 6) sts at beg of next 2 rows.
Leave rem 36 (40: 42: 46: 48) sts on a holder.

yoke

With right side facing and 5mm circular needle, work across right front, sleeve, back, sleeve and left front as follows: k21 (23: 24: 26: 28) sts from right front, k last st tog with first st of sleeve, k34 (38: 40: 44: 46), k last st tog with first st of back, k37 (41: 43: 47: 51), k last st with first st of sleeve, k34 (38: 40: 44: 46), k last st tog with first st of left front, k21 (23: 24: 26: 28). **151 (167: 175: 191: 203) sts.**
Work backwards and forwards in rows.
Next row K1, p to last st, k1.
Next row K18 (20: 21: 23: 25), k2tog, k3, skpo, k28 (32: 34: 38: 40), k2tog, k3, skpo, k31 (35: 37: 41: 45), k2tog, k3, skpo, k28 (32: 34: 38: 40), k2tog, k3, skpo, k18 (20: 21: 23: 25). **143 (159: 167: 183: 195) sts.**
Next row K1, p to last st, k1.
Next row K17 (19: 20: 22: 24), k2tog, k3, skpo, k26 (30: 32: 36: 38), k2tog, k3, skpo, k29 (33: 35: 39: 43), k2tog, k3, skpo, k26 (30: 32: 36: 38), k2tog, k3, skpo, k17 (19: 20: 22: 24). **135 (151: 159: 175: 187) sts.**
Next row K1, p to last st, k1.
Next row K16 (18: 19: 21: 23), k2tog, k3, skpo, k24 (28: 30: 34: 36), k2tog, k3, skpo, k27 (31: 33: 37: 41), k2tog, k3, skpo, k24 (28: 30: 34: 36), k2tog, k3, skpo, k16 (18: 19: 21: 23). **127 (143: 151: 167: 179) sts.**
Next row K1, p to last st, k1.
Next row K15 (17: 18: 20: 22), k2tog, k3, skpo, k22 (26: 28: 32: 34), k2tog, k3, skpo, k25 (29: 31: 35: 39), k2tog, k3, skpo, k22 (26: 28: 32: 34), k2tog, k3, skpo, k15 (17: 18: 20: 22). **119 (135: 143: 159: 171) sts.**
Cont in this way dec 8 sts on every right side row until 71 (79: 87: 95: 99) sts rem, ending with a wrong side row.

Buttonhole row K2, k2tog, y2rn, skpo, work to end, dec as set.

Next row Work to end, working twice in y2rn.

Work 4 (4: 6 :6: 6) more rows, dec on the next row and 1 (1: 2: 2: 2) foll right side rows as set. **47 (55: 55: 63: 67) sts.**

Shape hood

Next row (right side) K9 (10: 10: 12: 12), cast off next 29 (35: 35: 39: 43) sts, k to end.

Next row K1, p8 (9: 9: 11: 11), cast on 56 (60: 60: 66: 72) sts, p8 (9: 9: 11: 11), k1. **74 (80: 80: 90: 96) sts.**

Next row K to end.

Next row K1, p to last st, k1.

Rep the last 2 rows 18 (19: 21: 22: 23) times more.

Shape top

Next row K34 (37: 37: 42: 45), k2tog, k2, skpo, k34 (37: 37: 42: 45).

Next row K1, p32 (35: 35: 40: 43), p2tog tbl, p2, p2tog, p32 (35: 35: 40: 43), k1.

Next row K32 (35: 35: 40: 43), k2tog, k2, skpo, k32 (35: 35: 40: 43).

Next row K1, p30 (33: 33: 38: 41), p2tog tbl, p2, p2tog, p30 (33: 33: 38: 41), k1.

Next row K30 (33: 33: 38: 41), k2tog, k2, skpo, k30 (33: 33: 38: 41).

Next row K1, p28 (31: 31: 36: 39), p2tog tbl, p2, p2tog, p28 (31: 31: 36: 39), k1.

Next row K28 (31: 31: 36: 39), k2tog, k2, skpo, k28 (31: 31: 36: 39).

Next row K1, p26 (29: 29: 34: 37), p2tog tbl, p2, p2tog, p26 (29: 29: 34: 37), k1.

Cast off.

to make up   Join side and sleeve seams. Join underarm seam. Fold cast-off edge of hood in half and join seam. Easing in fullness, sew cast-on edge of hood to cast-off edge of back neck. Sew on button.

cable socks

sizes
To fit ages 3–6 months

materials
1 x 50g ball Debbie Bliss Cashmerino DK in lilac
Pair 4 mm knitting needles
Cable needle

tension
22 sts and 30 rows to 10 cm square over st st using 4 mm needles.

abbreviations
C4B = slip next 2 sts onto cable needle and hold to back of work, k2, then k2 from cable needle.
pfb = purl into front and back of next st.
See page 25.

sock (make 2)

With 4mm needles, cast on 42 sts.

1st row K2, * p1, k4, p1, k2; rep from * to end.

2nd row P2, * k1, p4, k1, p2; rep from * to end.

3rd row K2, * p1, C4B, p1, k2; rep from * to end.

4th row As 2nd row.

These 4 rows **form** the cable patt and are repeated once more then the first 3 rows again.

Ridge row K4, * k2tog, k6; rep from * to last 6 sts, k2tog, k4. **37 sts.**

Inc row * P2, k1, p1, pfb, p1, k1; rep from * to last 2 sts, p2. **42 sts.**

Beg with a 1st row, rep the 4 cable patt rows 4 times more, then rep the first 3 patt rows again.

1st dec row P2, * k1, p2tog, p2tog, k1, p2; rep from * to end. **32 sts.**

2nd dec row K3, * k2tog, k6; rep from * to last 5 sts, k2tog, k3. **28 sts.**

Shape heel
Next row P8, turn.

Work a further 9 rows in st st on these 8 sts only.

Dec row P2, p2tog, p1, turn.

Next row Sl 1, k3.

Dec row P3, p2tog, p1, turn.

Next row Sl 1, k4.

Dec row P4, p2tog.

Leave rem 5 sts on a holder.

With wrong side facing, slip centre 12 sts onto a holder, rejoin yarn to rem 8 sts, p to end.

Work a further 8 rows in st st on these 8 sts only.

Dec row K2, k2tog tbl, k1, turn.

Next row Sl 1, p3.

Dec row K3, k2tog tbl, k1, turn.

Next row Sl 1, p4.

Dec row K4, k2tog tbl, turn.

Next row Sl 1, p4.

Shape instep
Next row K5, pick up and k8 sts evenly along inside edge of heel, k12 sts from holder, pick up and k8 sts evenly along inside edge of heel, then k5 sts from holder. **38 sts.**

P 1 row.

Dec row K11, k2tog, k12, k2tog tbl, k11.

P 1 row.

Dec row K10, k2tog, k12, k2tog tbl, k10.

P 1 row.

Dec row K9, k2tog, k12, k2tog tbl, k9.

P 1 row.

Dec row K8, k2tog, k12, k2tog tbl, k8. **30 sts.**

Beg with a p row, work 13 rows in st st.

Shape toes
Dec row K1, [k2tog tbl, k5] 4 times, k1.

P 1 row.

Dec row K1, [k2tog tbl, k4] 4 times, k1.

P 1 row.

Dec row K1, [k2tog tbl, k3] 4 times, k1.

P 1 row.

Dec row K1, [k2tog tbl, k2] 4 times, k1. **14 sts.**

Dec row [P2tog] to end. **7 sts.**

Cast off.

to make up

Join seam across the toes, then cont to join seam along centre of sole and up the centre back, reversing seam on cuff. Turn cuff onto right side.

crossover vest 〔101〕

measurements

To fit ages 0–3 (3–6: 6–9: 9–12) months

finished measurements

Chest 42 (46: 50: 54)cm

Length to shoulder 26 (28: 30: 32)cm

Sleeve length 12 (13: 14: 16)cm

materials

2 (3: 3: 3) x 50g balls Debbie Bliss Baby Cashmerino in lilac (M) and a small amount in chocolate (C)

Pair each 3mm and 3.25mm knitting needles

60cm ribbon, 7mm wide

One small button

tension

25 sts and 34 rows to 10cm square over st st using 3.25mm needles.

abbreviations

See page 25.

back

With 3mm needles and C, cast on 65 (70: 75: 80) sts.
K 1 row.
Change to 3.25mm needles and M.
Beg with a k row, work in st st.
Work 6 (8: 10: 10) rows.
Dec row (right side) K8, skpo, k to last 10 sts, k2tog, k8.
Work 9 (9: 9: 11) rows.
Rep the last 10 (10: 10: 12) rows 3 times more and the dec row again. **55 (60: 65: 70) sts.**
Cont straight until back measures 17 (18: 20: 21)cm from cast-on edge, ending with a p row.
Shape armholes
Cast off 6 sts at beg of next 2 rows. **43 (48: 53: 58) sts.**
Cont straight until back measures 26 (28: 30: 32) cm from cast-on edge, ending with a p row.
Shape shoulders
Cast off 5 (6: 7: 8) sts at beg of next 4 rows.
Leave rem 23 (24: 25: 26) sts on a holder.

left front

With 3mm needles and C, cast on 44 (47: 50: 53) sts.
K 1 row.
Change to 3.25mm needles and M.
Beg with a k row, work in st st.
Work 6 (8: 10: 10) rows.
Dec row (right side) K8, skpo, k to end.
Work 9 (9: 9: 11) rows.
Rep the last 10 (10: 10: 12) rows 3 times more and the dec row again. **39 (42: 45: 48) sts.**
Cont straight until front measures 17 (18: 20: 21) cm from cast-on edge, ending with a p row.
Shape armhole
Cast off 6 sts at beg of next row. **33 (36: 39: 42) sts.**
Next row P to end.
Buttonhole row K to last 4 sts, yf, k2tog, k2.
Next row P to end.
Next row K to end.
Shape neck
Next row (wrong side) Cast off 5 (6: 7: 8) sts, p to end. **28 (30: 32: 34) sts.**
K 1 row.
Next row Cast off 5 sts, p to end.
K 1 row.
Next row Cast off 3 sts, p to end. **20 (22: 24: 26) sts.**
Next row K to last 2 sts, k2tog.
Cont to dec 1 st at neck edge on every foll right-side row until 10 (12: 14: 16) sts rem.
Cont straight until front measures same as Back to shoulder, ending at armhole edge.
Shape shoulder
Cast off 5 (6: 7: 8) sts at beg of next row.
Work 1 row.
Cast off rem 5 (6: 7: 8) sts.

right front

With 3 mm needles and C, cast on 44 (47: 50: 53) sts.
K 1 row.
Change to 3.25mm needles and M.
Beg with a k row, work in st st.
Work 6 (8: 10: 10) rows.
Dec row (right side) K to last 10 sts, k2tog, k8.
Work 9 (9: 9: 11) rows.
Rep the last 10 (10: 10: 12) rows 3 times more and the dec row again. **39 (42: 45: 48) sts.**
Cont straight until front measures 17 (18: 20: 21)cm from cast-on edge, ending with a k row.
Shape armhole
Cast off 6 sts at beg of next row. **33 (36: 39: 42) sts.**
Work 4 rows straight.
Shape neck
Next row (right side) Cast off 5 (6: 7: 8) sts, k to end. **28 (30: 32: 34) sts.**
P 1 row.
Next row Cast off 5 sts, k to end.
P 1 row.
Next row Cast off 3 sts, k to end. **20 (22: 24: 26) sts.**
P 1 row.
Next row Skpo, k to end.
Cont to dec 1 st at neck edge on every foll right-side row until 10 (12: 14: 16) sts rem.
Cont straight until front measures same as Back to shoulder, ending at armhole edge.
Shape shoulder
Cast off 5 (6: 7: 8) sts at beg of next row.
Work 1 row.
Cast off rem 5 (6: 7: 8) sts.

sleeves

With 3 mm needles and C, cast on 35 (38: 38: 41) sts.
K 1 row.
Change to 3.25mm needles and M.
Beg with a k row, work in st st and inc 1 st at each end of the 5th row and every foll 6th row until there are 45 (50: 50: 55) sts.
Cont straight until sleeve measures 12 (13: 14: 16)cm from cast-on edge, ending with a p row.
Mark each end of last row with a coloured thread.
Work a further 2 cm, ending with a p row.
Cast off.

button strip

With 3 mm needles and M, cast on 15 (17: 19: 21) sts.
K 1 row.
Cast off.

right front edging	With right side facing, 3mm needles and C, pick up and k53 (55: 61: 63) sts evenly along right front edge. K 1 row. Cast off.
left front edging	With right side facing, 3mm needles and C, pick up and k53 (55: 61: 63) sts evenly along left front edge. K 1 row. Cast off.
neckband	Join shoulder seams. With right side facing, 3mm needles and C, pick up and k1 st across row ends of right front band, 39 (42: 43: 46) sts up right front neck, k across 23 (24: 25: 26) sts from back neck holder, pick up and k39 (42: 43: 46) sts down left front neck then pick up and k1 st across row ends of front band. **103 (110: 113: 120) sts.** K 1 row. Cast off.
to make up	Sew sleeves into armholes with row ends above markers sewn to sts cast off at underarm. Join side and sleeve seams. Cut ribbon in half and sew one piece to right front and one on left front. Sew one end of button strip to right front armhole seam 4 rows above armhole shaping then sew button to other end.

measurements

To fit ages 0–3 (3–6: 6–9: 9–12) months

finished measurements

Over nappy 41 (46: 51: 56)cm

Length 29 (33: 38: 43)cm

materials

2 (2: 2: 3) x 50g balls Debbie Bliss Baby Cashmerino in chocolate (M) and small amount in lilac (C)

Pair each 3mm and 3.25mm knitting needles

Waist length of 1.5cm wide elastic

tension

25 sts and 34 rows to 10cm square over st st using 3.25mm needles.

abbreviations

See page 25.

106 trousers to match

legs (make 2)

With 3mm needles and C, cast on 54 (60: 66: 72) sts.

Rib row * K1, p1; rep from * to end.

Change to M and work a further 9 rows.

Change to 3.25mm needles.

Beg with a k row, work in st st until work measures 14 (16: 17: 19)cm from cast-on edge, ending with a p row.

Shape crotch

Inc 1 st at each end of the next row and 2 (2: 3: 3) foll alt rows.

P 1 row.

Cast on 3 sts at beg of next 2 rows. **66 (72: 80: 86) sts.**

Shape for legs

Work 2 rows.

Dec 1 st at each end of the next row and 2 (3: 4: 5) foll alt rows. **60 (64: 70: 74) sts.**

Dec 1 st at each end of 5 (6: 7: 8) foll 6th rows. **50 (52: 56: 58) sts.**

Work 6 (6: 8: 10) rows.

Change to 3mm needles and C.

K 2 rows.

Cast off.

to make up

Join inner leg seams. Join centre front and back seam. Join elastic into a ring. Work a herringbone casing over rib at waist, enclosing elastic.

sizes
To fit ages 3–6 (9–12: 18–24) months

materials
1 x 50g ball Debbie Bliss Cashmerino Aran in duck egg blue (A) and oddments in chocolate (B)
Pair each 4.50mm and 5mm knitting needles

tension
18 sts and 24 rows to 10cm square over st st using 5mm needles.
20 sts and 36 rows to 10cm square over garter st using 5mm needles.

abbreviations
See page 25.

pompon beret

to make

With 4.50mm needles and B, cast on 56 (64: 72) sts.
Rib row * K1, p1; rep from * to end.
This row **forms** the rib.
Change to A.
Work a further 5 rows in rib.
Change to 5mm needles.
K 4 rows.
Inc row K2, * m1, k4; rep from * to last 2 sts, m1, k2. 70 (80: 90) sts.
K 3 rows.
Inc row K2, * m1, k5; rep from * to last 3 sts, m1, k3. 84 (96: 108) sts.
K 13 rows.
Dec row K1, * skpo, k4; rep from * to last 5 sts, skpo, k3. 70 (80: 90) sts.
K 3 rows.
Dec row K1, * skpo, k3; rep from * to last 4 sts, skpo, k2. 56 (64: 72) sts.
K 3 rows.
Dec row K1, * skpo, k2; rep from * to last 3 sts, skpo, k1. 42 (48: 54) sts.
K 3 rows.
Dec row K1, * skpo, k1; rep from * to last 2 sts, skpo. 28 (32: 36) sts.
K 3 rows.
Dec row * Skpo; rep from * to end. 14 (16: 18) sts.
K 1 row.
Dec row * Skpo; rep from * to end. 7 (8: 9) sts.
Break yarn, thread end through rem sts, pull up and secure.

to finish

Join seam. Make a small pompon from B (see page 43) and sew to top of beret.

building blocks

size
Each block measures approximately 7.5 x 7.5 x 7.5cm

materials
1 x 50g ball Debbie Bliss Baby Cashmerino in each of indigo (A), duck egg (B), lime (C), raspberry (D), silver (E) and camel (F)
Oddments of brown yarn for embroidery
Pair 3mm knitting needles
5 foam blocks, each 7.5 x 7.5 x 7.5cm, or toy stuffing (see note below)

tension
26 sts and 36 rows over st st to 10cm square using 3mm needles.

abbreviations
See page 25.

note
Each of the five blocks of the building blocks set is made from six different knitted faces.
If you are using foam for the filling when making up the blocks, make sure you use
non-toxic EVA (closed cell) foam available from reputable foam suppliers.

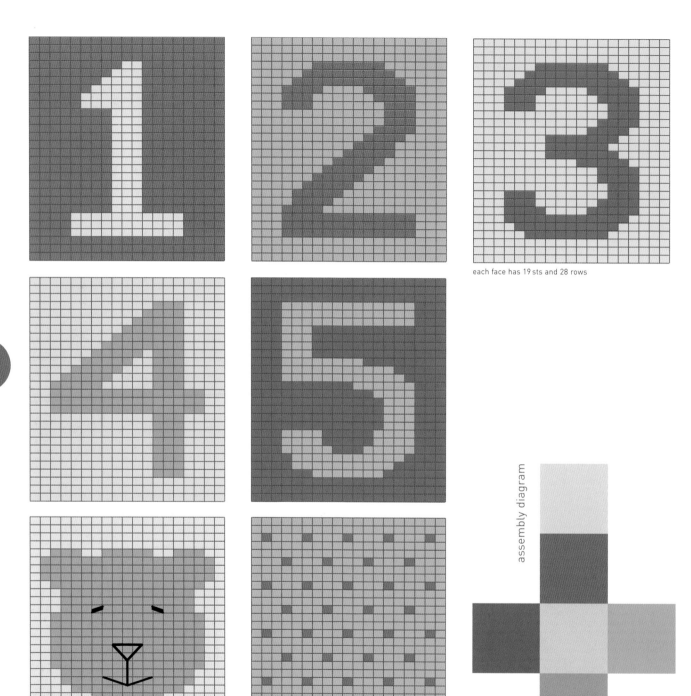

each face has 19 sts and 28 rows

assembly diagram

plain face
(make 5)

With 3mm needles and A, cast on 19 sts.
Moss st row K1, [p1, k1] to end.
Rep the moss st row 31 times more.
Cast off in moss st.
Make 4 more plain faces in same way, working one in each of B, C, D and E.

narrow stripe face (make 5)

With 3mm needles and A, cast on 19 sts.
Work in garter st stripe sequence as follows:
* K 1 row A, 2 rows B, 2 rows C, 2 rows D, 2 rows E, 2 rows F, 1 row A; rep from * twice more,
then k 1 row A, 2 rows B, 2 rows C, 1 row D.
Cast off knitwise in D.
Make 4 more narrow stripe faces in same way.

wide stripe face (make 5)

With 3mm needles and A, cast on 19 sts.
Beg with a k row, work 27 rows in st st in stripe sequence as follows:
3 rows A, 1 row B, 1 row A, 3 rows B, 1 row C, 1 row B, 3 rows C, 1 row D, 1 row C, 3 rows D,
1 row E, 1 row D, 3 rows E, 1 row F, 1 row E, 2 rows F.
Cast off knitwise in F.
Make 4 more wide stripe faces in same way.

bear face
(make 5)

With 3mm needles and E, cast on 19 sts.
Beg with a k row, work 28 rows in st st from bear chart, using E for background and F for bear.
Cast off purlwise.
Embroider eyes, snout and mouth with brown yarn.
Make 4 more bear faces in same way, using F for all the bears and A or E for background.

bird's-eye spot face (make 5)

With 3mm needles and background colour of your choice, cast on 19 sts.
Beg with a k row, work 28 rows in st st from bird's-eye spot chart using spot colour of your choice.
Cast off.
Make 4 more bird's-eye spot faces in same way, using a different colour combination for each one.

number face
(make 5)

With 3mm needles and background colour of your choice, cast on 19 sts.
Beg with a k row, work 28 rows in st st from number chart '1' using number colour of your choice.
Make 4 more number faces in same way, using a different number (2, 3, 4 and 5) and a different colour combination for each one.

to make up

For each of the five blocks, select one of each of the six different faces and sew them together as follows:
Join four faces together in a strip; then join the remaining two faces to the strip as shown in the assembly diagram opposite. Join the first face to the fourth face of the strip of four, then join the remaining three sides of one of the side faces to the four. Insert the foam block or fill with toy stuffing until firm and join the remaining three sides to the four.

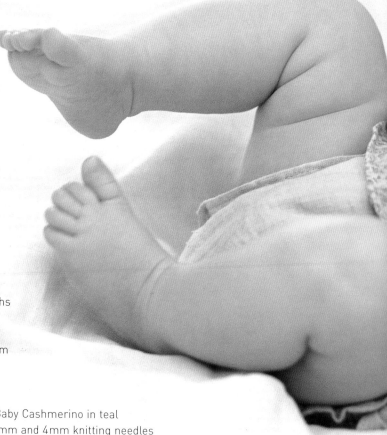

measurements

To fit ages 3–6 (6–9: 9–12) months
actual measurements
Chest 50 (53: 56) cm
Length to shoulder 26 (28: 30) cm
Sleeve length 15 (16: 17) cm

materials

3 (4: 4) x 50g balls Debbie Bliss Baby Cashmerino in teal
Pair each 2.75mm, 3.25mm, 3.75mm and 4mm knitting needles
1 m narrow ribbon

tension

25 sts and 34 rows to 10cm square over st st using 3.25mm needles.

abbreviations

sk2togpo = slip 1, k2tog, pass slipped st over.
See page 25.

note

When measuring the length from the cast-on edge, the measurement
should be taken along the length of the single st between eyelet holes.

matineecoat

back

With 4mm needles, cast on 81 (89: 97) sts.
1st row K1, * yf, k2, sk2togpo, k2, yf, k1; rep from * to end.
2nd row P to end.
Rep these 2 rows until back measures 6cm from cast-on edge (see Note) ending with a p row.
Change to 3.75mm needles and cont in patt until back measures 11 (12: 13)cm from cast-on edge, ending with a p row.
Change to 3.25mm needles and cont in patt until back measures 15 (16: 17)cm from cast-on edge, ending with a 1st row.
Dec row (wrong side) P10 (5: 2), p2tog, p1 (3: 1), [p2tog, p3 (1: 3), p2tog, p1 (3: 1)] 7 (9: 11) times, p2tog, p10 (5: 2). **65 (69: 73) sts.**
Beg with a k row, work in st st until back measures 26 (28: 30)cm, ending with a p row.
Shape shoulders
Cast off 20 (21: 22) sts at beg of next 2 rows.
Leave rem 25 (27: 29) sts on a holder.

left front

With 4mm needles, cast on 42 (50: 58) sts.
1st row K1, * yf, k2, sk2togpo, k2, yf, k1; rep from * to last st, k1.
2nd row P to end.
** Rep these 2 rows until front measures 6cm from cast-on edge, ending with a p row.
Change to 3.75mm needles and cont in patt until front measures 11 (12: 13)cm from cast-on edge, ending with a p row.
Change to 3.25mm needles and cont in patt until front measures 15 (16: 17)cm from cast-on edge, ending with a 1st row.
Dec row (wrong side) P and dec 8 (14: 20) sts evenly across row. **34 (36: 38) sts.**
K 1 row.
Shape neck
Cont in st st and cast off 2 sts at beg (neck edge) of next row and foll wrong side row, then dec 1 st at same edge of next 5 (6: 7) alt rows, then on every foll 4th row until 20 (21: 22) sts rem.
Cont straight until front measures same as Back to shoulder.
Cast off.

right front

With 4mm needles, cast on 42 (50: 58) sts.
1st row K2, * yf, k2, sk2togpo, k2, yf, k1: rep from * to end.
2nd row P to end.
Work exactly as for Left Front from ** to **.
Shape neck
Cast off 2 sts at (neck edge) of next row and foll right side row, then dec 1 st at same edge of next 5 (6: 7) alt rows, then on every foll 4th row until 20 (21: 22) sts rem.
Cont straight until front measures same as Back to shoulder.
Cast off.

sleeves

With 4mm needles, cast on 41 (41: 49) sts.
1st row K1, * yf, k2, sk2togpo, k2, yf, k1; rep from * to end.
2nd row P to end.
Rep these 2 rows 3 times more.
Change to 3.25mm needles.
Beg with a k row, work in st st, **at the same time**, inc 1 st at each end of the 5th row and 6 (9: 8) foll 5th (4th: 5th) rows. **55 (61: 67) sts.**
Cont straight until sleeve measures 15 (16: 17)cm, ending with a p row.
Cast off.

edgings

Join shoulder seams.
With right side facing and 2.75mm needles, pick up and k 44 (46: 48) sts up right front edge to start of neck shaping, 26 (28: 32) sts to shoulder, 25 (27: 29) sts across back neck, 26 (28: 32) sts down left front neck, then 44 (46: 48) sts down left front edge. **165 (175: 189) sts.**
Cast off knitwise.

to make up

Matching centre of cast-off edge of sleeve to shoulder, sew on sleeves. Join side and sleeve seams. Thread ribbon around back and front through last eyelet row before yoke, to tie at front.

118 cable yoke jacket

measurements

To fit ages 9–12 (12–18: 18–24) months

actual measurements

Chest 65 (69: 75)cm

Length to shoulder 30 (34: 38)cm

Sleeve length 16 (18: 23)cm

materials

6 (7: 8) x 50g balls Debbie Bliss Cotton Double Knitting in duck egg blue

Pair each 3.75mm and 4mm knitting needles

Cable needle

25 (25: 30)cm open-ended zip fastener

tension

20 sts and 28 rows to 10cm square over st st using 4mm needles.

abbreviations

C4F = slip next 2 sts onto cable needle and hold to front of work, k2, then k2 from cable needle.

pfb = purl into front and back of next st.

See page 25.

back

With 3.75mm needles, cast on 67 (71: 77) sts.

Moss st row K1, [p1, k1] to end.

Rep this row 3 times more.

Change to 4mm needles.

Beg with a k row, work in st st until back measures 16 (18: 20)cm from cast-on edge, ending with a k row.

Inc row P3 (5: 8), [pfb, p5] 10 times, pfb, p3 (5: 8). **78 (82: 88) sts.**

Yoke

1st row (right side) Moss st 2 (4: 7), [C4F, moss st 3] 10 times, c4f, moss st 2 (4: 7).

2nd row Moss st 2 (4: 7), [p4, moss st 3] 10 times, p4, moss st 2 (4: 7).

3rd row Moss st 2 (4: 7), [k4, moss st 3] 10 times, k4, moss st 2 (4: 7).

4th row As 2nd row.

Rep the last 4 rows until work measures 30 (34: 38)cm from cast-on edge, ending with a wrong side row.

Cast off all sts, working skpo across centre 2 sts of each cable.

left front

With 3.75mm needles, cast on 32 (34: 36) sts.

1st moss st row [P1, k1] to end.

2nd moss st row [K1, p1] to end.

Rep these 2 rows once more.

Change to 4mm needles and work as follows:

1st row K to last 3 sts, moss st 3.

2nd row Moss st 3, p to end.

Rep the last 2 rows until work measures 16 (18: 20)cm from cast-on edge, ending with a right side row.

Inc row Moss st 3, p1, [pfb, p5] 4 times, pfb, p3 (5: 7) and inc 1 st in last st of 3rd size only. **37 (39: 42) sts.**

Yoke

1st row (right side) Moss st 2 (4: 7), [C4F, moss st 3] 5 times.

2nd row Moss st 3, [p4, moss st 3] 4 times, p4, moss st 2 (4: 7).

3rd row Moss st 2 (4: 7), [k4, moss st 3] 5 times.

4th row As 2nd row.

Rep the last 4 rows until front measures 25 (28: 32)cm, ending with a wrong side row.

Shape neck

Next row Patt 34 (36: 39) and slip rem 3 sts onto a safety pin for collar.

Next row (wrong side) Cast off the 4 sts of cable working p2tog tbl on centre 2 sts, patt to end.

Patt 1 row.

Next row Cast off 3 sts, patt to end.

Now dec 1 st at neck edge on next 5 rows. **22 (24: 27) sts.**

Work a few rows in patt until front measures 30 (34: 38)cm, ending with a wrong side row.

Cast off all sts, working skpo across centre 2 sts of each cable.

right front

With 3.75mm needles, cast on 32 (34: 36) sts.

1st moss st row [K1, p1] to end.

2nd moss st row [P1, k1] to end.

Rep these 2 rows once more.

Change to 4mm needles and work as follows:

1st row Moss st 3, k to end.

2nd row P to last 3 sts, moss st 3.

Rep the last 2 rows until front measures 16 (18: 20)cm from cast-on edge, ending with a right side row.

1st and 2nd sizes only

Inc row P3 (5), [pfb, p5] 4 times, pfb, p1, moss st 3. **37 (39) sts.**

3rd size only

Inc row Inc in first st, p6, [pfb, p5] 4 times, pfb, p1, moss st 3. **42 sts.**

All sizes

Yoke

1st row (right side) [Moss st 3, C4F] 5 times, moss st 2 (4: 7).

2nd row Moss st 2 (4: 7), [p4, moss st 3] 5 times.

3rd row [Moss st 3, k4] 5 times, moss st 2 (4: 7).

4th row As 2nd row.

Rep the last 4 rows until front measures 25 (28: 32)cm, ending with a wrong side row.

Shape neck

Next row Moss st 3 and slip these sts onto a safety pin for collar, cast off next 4 sts of cable working skpo on centre 2 sts, then patt to end.

Patt 1 row.

Next row Cast off 3, patt to end.

Patt 1 row, then dec 1 st at neck edge of next 5 rows. **22 (24: 27) sts.**

Work a few rows in patt until work measures 30 (34: 38)cm, ending with a wrong side row.

Cast off all sts, working skpo across centre 2 sts of each cable.

sleeves

With 3.75mm needles, cast on 31 (33: 35) sts.

Moss st row K1, [p1, k1] to end.

Rep this row 3 times more.

Inc row (right side) K all sts and inc 4 (4: 6) sts evenly across row. **35 (37: 41) sts.**

Change to 4mm needles.

Beg with a p row, work in st st and inc 1 st at each end of 4th (4th: 2nd) and every foll 4th (4th: 6th) row until there are 51 (55: 59) sts.

Cont straight until sleeve measures 16 (18: 23)cm from cast-on edge, ending with a p row.

Cast off.

collar

Join shoulder seams.
With right side facing and 3.75mm needles, slip 3 sts from right front safety pin onto needle, join on yarn and pick up and k 15 (16: 17) sts up right front neck, 29 (31: 33) sts across back neck, 15 (16: 17) sts down left front neck, then moss st across 3 sts from left front safety pin. 65 (69: 73) sts.
Moss st 1 row as set by sts from safety pins.
Next 2 rows Moss st to last 21 sts, turn.
Next 2 rows Moss st to last 16 sts, turn.
Next 2 rows Moss st to last 11 sts, turn.
Next 2 rows Moss st to last 6 sts, turn.
Next row Moss st across all sts.
Moss st 10 rows.
Cast off in moss st.

to make up

With centre of cast-off edge of sleeve to shoulder, sew on sleeves. Join side and sleeve seams.
Hand-sew zip to fronts with zipper tape sewn behind moss st edge.

measurements

To fit ages 6 (12: 18: 24) months
finished measurements
Chest 59 (63: 67: 71) cm
Length to shoulder 42 (48: 54: 60) cm
Sleeve length (with cuff turned back) 16 (18: 21: 24) cm

materials

11 (12: 14: 15) x 50g balls Debbie Bliss Cotton DK in pink (M) and 1 x 50g ball in chocolate (C)
Pair each 3.75mm and 4mm knitting needles
4mm circular knitting needle

tension

20 sts and 32 rows to 10cm square over moss st using 4mm needles.

abbreviations

See page 25.

bath robe

back

With 4mm circular needle and M, cast on 157 (169: 185: 197) sts.
Moss st row K1, * p1, k1; rep from * to end.
This row **forms** the moss st and is repeated.
Work a further 31 (33: 35: 37) rows in moss st.
Dec row (right side) Moss st 42 (44: 46: 48), k3tog, moss st to last 45 (47: 49: 51), k3tog, moss st to end.
Moss st 13 rows.
Dec row (right side) Moss st 41 (43: 45: 47), p3tog, moss st to last 44 (46: 48: 50), p3tog, moss st to end.
Moss st 13 rows.
Cont in moss st, dec 4 sts as set on next row and 2 (3: 4: 5) foll 14th rows, so ending with the dec row. **137 (145: 157: 165) sts.**
Work 11 rows.
Divide for back and fronts
Next row Moss st 36 (38: 41: 43) sts and leave these sts on a holder for right front, cast off next 6 (6: 8: 8) sts, with 1 st on needle after cast-off, moss st next 52 (56: 58: 62) sts and leave these sts on a holder for back, cast off next 6 (6: 8: 8) sts, with 1 st on needle after cast-off, moss st 35 (37: 40: 42).
Working on the last set of 36 (38: 41: 43) sts for left front, work in moss st for a further 11 (12: 13: 14) cm, ending with a wrong-side row.
Shape shoulder
Cast off 16 (17: 18: 19) sts at beg of next row.
Work 1 row.
Leave rem 20 (21: 23: 24) sts on a spare needle.
Back
With wrong side facing, rejoin yarn to 53 (57: 59: 63) sts on back holder, patt to end.
Work straight until back measures same as Left Front to shoulder, ending with a wrong-side row.
Shape shoulders
Cast off 16 (17: 18: 19) sts at beg of next 2 rows.
Cast off rem 21 (23: 23: 25) sts.
Right front
With wrong side facing, rejoin yarn to 36 (38: 41: 43) sts on right front holder, patt to end.
Work straight until front measures same as Back to shoulder, ending with a right-side row.
Shape shoulder
Cast off 16 (17: 18: 19) sts at beg of next row. **20 (21: 23: 24) sts.**
Leave rem sts on a holder.

sleeves

With 4mm needles and C, cast on 29 (31: 33: 35) sts.
K 1 row.
Change to M.
Next row K1, * p1, k1; rep from * to end.
This row forms the moss st and is repeated.
Work a further 13 (13: 15: 15) rows in moss st.
Change to 3.75mm needles.
Work 14 (14: 16: 16) rows.
Change to 4mm needles.
Cont in moss st and inc 1 st at each end of 3rd (5th: 5th: 7th) row and every foll 4th row until

there are 45 (49: 55: 59) sts, taking all inc sts into moss st.
Cont straight until sleeve measures 20 (22: 26: 29) cm from cast-on edge, ending with a wrong-side row.
Mark each end of last row with a coloured thread.
Work a further 6 (6: 8: 8) rows.
Cast off.

hood

Join shoulder seams.
Using 4mm needles and M, cont as follows:
Next row (right side) Moss st 20 (21: 23: 24) sts from right front, cast on 31 (35: 35: 39) sts, moss st 20 (21: 23: 24) sts from left front. **71 (77: 81: 87) sts.**
Work 60 (62: 64: 66) rows in moss st.
Shape top
Next row Moss st 34 (37: 39: 42), work 3 tog, moss st 34 (37: 39: 42).
Next row Moss st 33 (36: 38: 41), work 3 tog, moss st 33 (36: 38: 41).
Next row Moss st 32 (35: 37: 40), work 3 tog, moss st 32 (35: 37: 40).
Next row Moss st 31 (34: 36: 39), work 3 tog, moss st 31 (34: 36: 39).
Next row Moss st 30 (33: 35: 38), work 3 tog, moss st 30 (33: 35: 38).
Next row Moss st 29 (32: 34: 37), work 3 tog, moss st 29 (32: 34: 37).
Next row Moss st 28 (31: 33: 36), work 3 tog, moss st 28 (31: 33: 36).
Next row Moss st 27 (30: 32: 35), work 3 tog, moss st 27 (30: 32: 35).
Cast off.

pockets (make 2)

With 4mm needles and M, cast on 19 (21: 21: 23) sts.
Work 24 (26: 26: 28) rows in moss st.
Change to C.
K 1 row.
Cast off in C.

tie belt

With 4mm circular needle and M, cast on 191 (201: 211: 221) sts.
Work 3 rows in moss st.
Cast off in moss st.

to make up

Join upper hood seam. Stitch cast-on edge of hood to sts cast-off at back neck. Join sleeve seams to markers, reversing seam for turn-up. Sew sleeves into armholes, with row ends above markers sewn to sts cast off at underarm. Sew on pockets.

first coat

measurements

To fit ages 0–3 (3–6: 6–9: 9–12) months

finished measurements

Chest 46 (50: 55: 60)cm

Length to shoulder 28 (30: 32: 34)cm

Sleeve length 12 (13: 14: 16)cm

materials

3 (3: 4: 4) x 50g balls Debbie Bliss Baby Cashmerino in stone (M) and a small amount in ecru (C)

Pair each 3mm and 3.25mm knitting needles

4 small buttons

tension

25 sts and 34 rows to 10cm square over st st and 32 sts and 34 rows to 10cm square over rib both using 3.25mm needles.

abbreviations

See page 25.

back

With 3mm needles and M, cast on 75 (83: 91: 99) sts.

K 3 rows.

Change to 3.25mm needles.

Beg with a k row, work in st st until back measures 15 (16: 18: 19)cm from cast-on edge, ending with a p row.

Next row (right side) K1, * p1, k1; rep from * to end.

Next row P1, * k1, p1; rep from * to end.

Rep the last 2 rows until back measures 18 (19: 22: 23)cm from cast-on edge, ending with a wrong-side row.

Shape armholes

Cast off 8 sts at beg of next 2 rows. **59 (67: 75: 83) sts.**

Dec 1 st at each end of the next row and 3 (4: 5: 6) foll alt rows. **51 (57: 63: 69) sts.**

Cont straight until back measures 28 (30: 32: 34)cm from cast-on edge, ending with a wrong-side row.

Shape shoulders

Cast off 9 (11: 14: 16) sts at beg of next 2 rows.

Leave rem 33 (35: 35: 37) sts on a holder.

left front

With 3mm needles and M, cast on 39 (43: 47: 51) sts.

K 3 rows.

Change to 3.25mm needles.

Next row (right side) K to end.

Next row K3, p to end.

These 2 rows form the st st with garter st edging.

Cont straight until front measures 15 (16: 18: 19)cm from cast-on edge, ending with a wrong-side row.

Next row (right side) * P1, k1; rep from * to last 5 sts, p1, k4.

Next row K3, * p1, k1; rep from * to end.

Rep the last 2 rows until front measures 18 (19: 22: 23)cm from cast-on edge, ending with a wrong-side row.

Shape armhole

Cast off 9 sts at beg of next row. **30 (34: 38: 42) sts.**

Work 1 row.

Dec 1 st at beg of the next row and 3 (4: 5: 6) foll alt rows. **26 (29: 32: 35) sts.**

Work straight until front measures 24 (26: 27: 29)cm from cast-on edge, ending with a wrong-side row.

Shape neck

Next row Rib to last 10 sts, leave these sts on a holder.

Dec 1 st at neck edge on every row until 9 (11: 14: 16) sts rem.

Cont straight until front measures same as Back to shoulder, ending at armhole edge.

Shape shoulder

Cast off.

Mark positions for 4 buttons, the first on the 3rd row of rib patt and the fourth 1cm below neck shaping, with the rem 2 buttons spaced evenly between.

  right front

With 3mm needles and M, cast on 39 (43: 47: 51) sts.

K 3 rows.

Change to 3.25mm needles.

Next row (right side) K to end.

Next row P to last 3 sts, k3.

These 2 rows form the st st with garter st edging.

Cont straight until front measures 15 (16: 18: 19)cm from cast-on edge, ending with a wrong-side row.

Next row (right side) K4, p1, * k1, p1; rep from * to end.

Next row K1, * p1, k1; rep from * to last 4 sts, p1, k3.

Buttonhole row K2, yf, k2tog, p1, rib to end.

Work rem buttonholes as set by this row to match button markers.

Rep the last 2 rows until front measures 18 (19: 22: 23)cm from cast-on edge, ending with a right-side row.

Shape armhole

Cast off 9 sts at beg of next row. **30 (34: 38: 42) sts.**

Dec 1 st at beg of the next row and 3 (4: 5: 6) foll alt rows. **26 (29: 32: 35) sts.**

Work straight until front measures 24 (26: 27: 29)cm from cast-on edge, ending with a wrong-side row.

Shape neck

Next row Rib 10 sts, leave these sts on a holder, rib to end.

Dec 1 st at neck edge on every row until 9 (11: 14: 16) sts rem.

Cont straight until front measures same as Back to shoulder, ending at armhole edge.

Shape shoulder

Cast off.

sleeves

With 3mm needles and M, cast on 40 (43: 45: 46) sts.
K 3 rows.
Change to 3.25mm needles.
Beg with a k row, work in st st and inc 1 st at each end of the 5th row and every foll 6th row until there are 50 (55: 57: 60) sts.
Cont straight until sleeve measures 12 (13: 14: 16)cm from cast-on edge, ending with a p row.
Mark each end of last row with a coloured thread.
Work a further 2cm, ending with a p row.
Shape top
Dec 1 st at each end of the next row and 3 (4: 5: 6) foll alt rows. **42 (45: 45: 46) sts.**
Cast off.

collar

Join shoulder seams.
With right side facing, 3.25mm needles and M, slip 10 sts from right front holder onto a needle, pick up and k16 (16: 18: 18) sts up right front neck, k33 (35: 35: 37) sts from back, 16 (16: 18: 18) sts down left side of front neck, k10 sts from left front holder. **85 (87: 91: 93) sts.**
Next row (wrong side) K1, * p1, k1; rep from * to end.
This row sets the rib.
Next 2 rows Rib to last 26 sts, turn.
Next 2 rows Rib to last 20 sts, turn.
Next 2 rows Rib to last 14 sts, turn.
Next 2 rows Rib to last 8 sts, turn.
Next row Rib to end.
Cast off 4 sts at beg of next 2 rows.
Work a further 14 (16: 16: 18) rows.
Break off yarn.
With right side facing, 3mm needles and M, pick up and k12 (14: 14: 16) sts along row ends of collar, k across sts of collar, then pick up and k12 (14: 14: 16) sts along row ends of collar.
Next row K12 (14: 14: 16), m1, k to last 12 (14: 14: 16) sts, m1, k to end.
Change to C.
Next row K to end.
Next row K12 (14: 14: 16), m1, k to last 12 (14: 14: 16) sts, m1, k to end.
Cast off.

to make up

Sew sleeves into armholes, with row ends above markers sewn to sts cast off at underarm. Join side and sleeve seams. Sew on buttons. Sew row ends of collar edging in place.

reversible
blanket

size
Approximately 100 x 100 cm

materials
13 x 50g balls Debbie Bliss Cashmerino Aran in each of stone (A) and blue (B)
1 x 50g ball Debbie Bliss Cashmerino Aran in chocolate (C) for blanket stitch detail
5mm circular knitting needle

tension
18 sts and 24 rows to 10cm square over st st using 5mm needles.

abbreviations
See page 25.

first side

With 5mm circular needle and A, cast on 175 sts.
Working back and forth in rows throughout, k 5 rows.
Work in patt as follows:
1st row (right side) K7, [p1, k7] to last 8 sts, p1, k7.
2nd row K3, p3, [k1, p1, k1, p5] to last 9 sts, k1, p1, k1, p3, k3.
3rd row K5, [p1, k3] to last 6 sts, p1, k5.
4th row K3, p1, [k1, p5, k1, p1] to last 3 sts, k3.
5th row K3, p1, [k7, p1] to last 3 sts, k3.
6th row As 4th row.
7th row As 3rd row.
8th row As 2nd row.
These 8 rows form the patt with garter st edging.
Cont in patt until work measures 98cm from cast-on edge, ending with a right side row.
K 5 rows.
Cast off.

second side

With 5mm circular needle and B, cast on 175 sts.
Working back and forth in rows throughout, k 5 rows.
Beg patt as follows:
1st row (right side) K3, [p1, k7] to last 4 sts, p1, k3.
2nd row K3, [p7, k1] to last 4 sts, p1, k3.
3rd row K5, [p1, k7] to last 10 sts, p1, k9.
4th row K3, p5, [k1, p7] to last 7 sts, k1, p3, k3.
5th row K7, [p1, k7] to end.
6th row K3, p3, [k1, p7] to last 9 sts, k1, p5, k3.
7th row K9, [p1, k7] to last 6 sts, p1, k5.
8th row K3, p1, [k1, p7] to last 3 sts, k3.
These 8 rows form the patt with garter st edging.
Cont in patt until work measures 98cm from cast-on edge, ending with a right side row.
K 5 rows.
Cast off.

to make up

With wrong sides together, join first and second sides together around the outer edge.

to finish

With two strands of C held together, work blanket stitch around the edges.

bootees
with blanket stitch detail

size
To fit ages 3–6 months

materials
1 x 50g ball Debbie Bliss Baby Cashmerino in pale blue (A) and oddments of chocolate (B) for blanket stitch detail
Pair 2.75mm knitting needles

tension
28 sts and 50 rows to 10cm square over garter st using 2.75mm needles.

abbreviations
See page 25.

boots (make 2)

With 2.75mm needles and A, cast on 36 sts.
K 36 rows.
Shape instep
Next row K23, turn.
Next row K10, turn.
Work 24 rows in garter st on centre 10 sts.
Next row K1, skpo, k to last 3 sts, k2tog, k1.
K 1 row.
Cut yarn.
With right side facing, rejoin yarn at base of instep and pick up and k13 sts along side of instep, k across centre 8 sts, then pick up and k13 sts along other side of instep. **34 sts.**
Beg with a p row, work 5 rows in st st on these 34 sts.
Next row [K next st tog with corresponding st 5 rows below] 34 times, then k to end.
Next row K to end. **60 sts.**
K 12 rows.
Beg with a k row, work 7 rows in st st.
Next row [P next st tog with corresponding st 7 rows below] to end.
Break off yarn.
Shape sole
Next row Slip first 25 sts onto right-hand needle, rejoin yarn and k10 sts, turn.
Next row K9, k2tog, turn.
Rep last row until 20 sts rem.
Cast off.

to finish

Join back seam. With back seam to centre of cast-off edge, join heel seam.
With B, work blanket stitch around edge of turnover.

rabbit
with blanket stitch detail

size
Approximately 25cm high

materials
2 x 50g balls Debbie Bliss Baby Cashmerino in pale blue (A), and oddments in each of chocolate (B) for embroidery and ecru (C) for pompon tail
Pair 2.75mm knitting needles
Washable toy stuffing (see Note on page 57)
10cm square of chocolate felt

tension
28 sts and 58 rows to 10cm square over garter st using 2.75mm needles.

abbreviations
ytb = yarn to back of work between two needles.
ytf = yarn to front of work between two needles.
s2togkpo = slip 2 sts tog, k1, pass 2 slipped sts over.
Also see page 25.

body back

(Worked from neck edge)
With 2.75mm needles and A, cast on 12 sts and k 1 row.
Shape shoulders
Next row [K2, m1] twice, k4, [m1, k2] twice. **16 sts.**
K 1 row.
Next row K3, m1, k2, m1, k6, m1, k2, m1, k3. **20 sts.**
K 5 rows.
Next row K1, m1, k to last st, m1, k1. **22 sts.**
K 5 rows. **
Rep the last 6 rows 5 times more. **32 sts.**
Shape base
Next row K1, [ssk, k11, k2tog] twice, k1. **28 sts.**
K 1 row.
Next row K1, [ssk, k9, k2tog] twice, k1. **24 sts.**
K 1 row.
*** Next row K1, [ssk, k7, k2tog] twice, k1. **20 sts.**
K 1 row.
Cont to dec 4 sts in this way on every alt row until 8 sts rem.
Next row K1, sl 1, k2tog, psso, k3tog, k1. **4 sts.**
Next row [K2tog] twice. **2 sts.**
Next row K2tog and fasten off.

body front

Work as Body Back to **.
Next row K1, m1, k to last st, m1, k1. **24 sts.**
K 5 rows.
Next row K1, m1, k10, m1, k2, m1, k10, m1, k1. **28 sts.**
K 5 rows.
Next row K1, m1, k10, m1, k6, m1, k10, m1, k1. **32 sts.**
K 5 rows.
Next row K1, m1, k to last st, m1, k1. **34 sts.**
K 5 rows.
Rep the last 6 rows once more. **36 sts.**
Next row K1, ssk, k6, [ssk, k5, k2tog] twice, k6, k2tog, k1. **30 sts.**
K 1 row.
Next row K1, ssk, k5, [ssk, k3, k2tog] twice, k5, k2tog, k1. **24 sts.**
K 1 row.
Now work as Body Back from *** to end.

head

With 2.75mm needles and A, cast on 4 sts.
1st row K.
2nd row K1, [m1, k1] to end. **7 sts.**
Rep the last 2 rows once more. **13 sts.**
5th, 7th, 9th and 11th rows K.
6th row [K1, m1, k5, m1] twice, k1. **17 sts.**
8th row K1, m1, k6, m1, k3, m1, k6, m1, k1. **21 sts.**
10th row K1, m1, k7, m1, k5, m1, k7, m1, k1. **25 sts.**
12th row K1, m1, k8, m1, k7, m1, k8, m1, k1. **29 sts.**
K 2 rows.
15th row K2, [ssk, k1] 3 times, k8, [k2tog, k1] 3 times, k1. **23 sts.**
16th row K4, m1, k3, m1, k9, m1, k3, m1, k4. **27 sts.**
K 3 rows.
20th row [K4, m1] twice, k11, [m1, k4] twice. **31 sts.**
K 3 rows.
24th row K4, m1, k5, m1, k13, m1, k5, m1, k4. **35 sts.**
K 1 row.
26th row K4, m1, k6, m1, k15, m1, k6, m1, k4. **39 sts.**
K 1 row.
28th row K4, m1, k7, m1, k17, m1, k7, m1, k4. **43 sts.**
K 1 row.
30th row K3, [m1, k4] 3 times, m1, k13, m1, [k4, m1] 3 times, k3. **51 sts.**
K 12 rows.
43rd row K9, k2tog, [k8, k2tog] 4 times. **46 sts.**
K 1 row.
45th row K8, k2tog, [k7, k2tog] 4 times. **41 sts.**
K 1 row.
47th row K7, k2tog, [k6, k2tog] 4 times. **36 sts.**
K 1 row.

Dec 5 sts in this way on next row and 4 foll alt rows. **11 sts.**
K 1 row.
Next row Sl 1, k2tog, psso, [k2tog] 4 times. **5 sts.**
Break yarn, thread through rem sts, pull up and secure.
Join seam, leaving a gap. Stuff carefully and close gap in seam.

ears (make 2)

With 2.75mm needles and A, cast on 15 sts.
K 1 row.
** Next 2 rows K2, ytf, sl 1, turn, ytf, sl 1, ytb, k2.
Next 2 rows K4, ytf, sl 1, turn, ytf, sl 1, ytb, k4.
Next 2 rows K6, ytf, sl 1, turn, ytf, sl 1, ytb, k6.
Next 2 rows K7, ytf, sl 1, turn, ytf, sl 1, ytb, k7.
K 1 row across all sts. ******
Rep from ** to ** once more.
K 48 rows.
Next row K1, skpo, k to last 3 sts, k2tog, k1.
K 3 rows.
Rep the last 4 rows once more. **11 sts.**
Next row K1, skpo, k to last 3 sts, k2tog, k1.
K 1 row.
Rep the last 2 rows twice more. **5 sts.**
Next row K1, s2togkpo, k1.
Next row S2togkpo and fasten off.
Fold cast-on edge in half and join.
With B, work blanket st around edge of each ear.

legs (make 2)

With 2.75mm needles and A, cast on 15 sts.
K 1 row.
2nd row K1, m1, k4, m1, k1, m1, k3, m1, k1, m1, k4, m1, k1. **21 sts.**
K 1 row.
4th row K1, m1, k6, m1, k2, m1, k3, m1, k2, m1, k6, m1, k1. **27 sts.**
K 1 row.
6th row K9, m1, k3, [m1, k1] 3 times, m1, k3, m1, k9. **33 sts.**
K 9 rows.
16th row K12, ssk, k5, k2tog, k12. **31 sts.**
K 1 row.
18th row K12, ssk, k3, k2tog, k12. **29 sts.**
K 1 row.
20th row K12, ssk, k1, k2tog, k12. **27 sts.**
K 1 row.
22nd row K11, ssk, k1, k2tog, k11. **25 sts.**
K 1 row.
24th row K10, ssk, k1, k2tog, k10. **23 sts.**
K 1 row.

26th row K9, ssk, k1, k2tog, k9. **21 sts.**
K 29 rows.
56th row K4, ssk, k9, k2tog, k4. **19 sts.**
K 1 row.
58th row K4, ssk, k7, k2tog, k4. **17 sts.**
K 1 row.
60th row K2, ssk, k2tog, k5, ssk, k2tog, k2. **13 sts.**
K 1 row.
62nd row K1, ssk, k2tog, s2togkpo, ssk, k2tog, k1. **7 sts.**
K 1 row.
64th row K1, ssk, k1, k2tog, k1. **5 sts.**
Break yarn, thread through rem sts, pull up and secure.

arms (make 2)

With 2.75mm needles and A, cast on 7 sts.
K 1 row.
2nd row [K1, m1, k2, m1] twice, k1. **11 sts.**
K 1 row.
4th row K1, m1, [k3, m1] 3 times, k1. **15 sts.**
K 1 row.
6th row K1, m1, k4, m1, k5, m1, k4, m1, k1. **19 sts.**
K 1 row.
8th row K1, m1, k17, m1, k1. **21 sts.**
K 1 row.
10th row K1, m1, k7, ssk, k1, k2tog, k7, m1, k1. **21 sts.**
K 1 row.
Rep the last 2 rows once more.
14th row K8, ssk, k1, k2tog, k8. **19 sts.**
K 1 row.
16th row K7, ssk, k1, k2tog, k7. **17 sts.**
K 24 rows.
41st row K2, ssk, k2tog, k5, ssk, k2tog, k2. **13 sts.**
K 1 row.
43rd row K1, ssk, k2tog, s2togkpo, ssk, k2tog, k1. **7 sts.**
K 1 row.
45th row K1, ssk, k1, k2tog, k1. **5 sts.**
Break yarn, thread through rem sts, pull up and secure.

to make up

Join body back to body front leaving neck edge open. Stuff firmly and run a thread around neck edge, pull up slightly and secure. Sew ears to head. Embroider facial features with B. Sew head to body at neck. Fold each arm and each leg in half, join seam leaving a gap, stuff firmly and close gap. Sew arms and legs in place to body. Using the little bear sole template on page 120, cut two soles from chocolate felt and sew to feet. With B, work 'toes' and 'paws' on feet and arms. Make a small pompon in C and sew to body.

daisycardigan

measurements

To fit ages 0–3 (3–6: 6–9: 9–12: 12–18: 18–24) months

actual measurements

Chest 49 (53: 57: 61: 65: 69)cm

Length to shoulder 21 (24: 26: 28: 32: 36)cm

Sleeve length 13 (15: 17: 19: 22: 24)cm

materials

5 (5: 6: 6: 7: 8) x 50g balls Debbie Bliss Cotton Double Knitting in pale green

Oddments of contrast yarn for embroidery

Pair each 3.25mm and 4mm knitting needles

5 (6: 6: 6: 7: 7) buttons

tension

20 sts and 32 rows to 10cm square over moss st using 4mm needles.

abbreviations

See page 25.

back

With 3.25mm needles, cast on 51 (55: 59: 63: 67: 71) sts.
K 5 rows.
Change to 4mm needles.
Moss st row * P1, k1; rep from * to last st, p1.
This row forms moss st and is repeated.
Work 3 more rows.
Eyelet row Moss st 1 (3: 5: 1: 3: 5), yrn, p2tog, * moss st 4, yrn, p2tog; rep from * to last
0 (2: 4: 0: 2: 4) sts, moss st 0 (2: 4: 0: 2: 4).
Cont in moss st until back measures 12 (14: 15: 16: 19: 22)cm from cast-on edge, ending with
a wrong side row.

Shape armholes

Cast off 4 sts at beg of next 2 rows. **43 (47: 51: 55: 59: 63)** sts.
Cont straight until back measures 21 (24: 26: 28: 32: 36)cm from cast-on edge, ending with
a wrong side row.

Shape shoulders

Cast off 10 (11: 13: 14: 16: 17) sts at beg of next 2 rows.
Cast off rem 23 (25: 25: 27: 27: 29) sts.

left front

With 3.25mm needles, cast on 28 (30: 32: 34: 36: 38) sts.
K 5 rows.
Change to 4mm needles.
1st row (right side) * P1, k1; rep from * to last 6 sts, p1, k5.
2nd row K5, p1, * k1, p1; rep from * to end.
These 2 rows form the moss st patt with garter st border.
Work 2 more rows.
Eyelet row Moss st 1 (3: 5: 1: 3: 5), yrn, p2tog, * moss st 4, yrn, p2tog; rep from * to last 7 sts, k1,
p1, k5.
Cont in moss st with garter st border until front measures 12 (14: 15: 16: 19: 22)cm from cast-on
edge, ending with a wrong side row.

Shape armhole

Cast off 4 sts at beg of next row. **24 (26: 28: 30: 32: 34)** sts.
Cont straight until front measures 17 (20: 21: 23: 26: 30)cm from cast-on edge, ending with a
wrong side row.

Shape neck

Next row Patt to last 7 (7: 8: 8: 9: 9) sts, leave these sts on a holder for collar.
Dec 1 st at neck edge on every row until 10 (11: 13: 14: 16: 17) sts rem.
Cont straight until front measures same as Back to shoulder, ending at armhole edge.

Shape shoulder

Cast off.
Mark position for 5 (6: 6: 6: 7: 7) buttons, the first on the eyelet row, the last 1cm below neck edge,
with the rem 3 (4: 4: 4: 5: 5) spaced evenly between.

right front

With 3.25mm needles, cast on 28 (30: 32: 34: 36: 38) sts.
K 5 rows.
Change to 4mm needles.
1st row (right side) K5, p1, * k1, p1; rep from * to end.
2nd row * P1, k1; rep from * to last 6 sts, p1, k5.
These 2 rows **form** the moss st patt with garter st border.
Work 2 more rows.
Eyelet and buttonhole row (right side) K1, k2tog, yf, k2, p1, k1, yf, skpo, * moss st 4, yf, skpo; rep from * to last 1 (3: 5: 1: 3: 5) sts, moss st 1 (3: 5: 1: 3: 5) sts.
Cont in moss st with garter st border, working buttonholes to match left front markers, until front measures 12 (14: 15: 16: 19: 22)cm from cast-on edge, ending with a right side row.
Shape armhole
Cast off 4 sts at beg of next row. **24 (26: 28: 30: 32: 34) sts.**
Cont straight until front measures 17 (20: 21: 23: 26: 30)cm from cast-on edge, ending with a wrong side row.
Shape neck
Next row Patt 7 (7: 8: 8: 9: 9) sts and leave these sts on a holder for collar, patt to end.
Dec 1 st at neck edge on every row until 10 (11: 13: 14: 16: 17) sts rem.
Cont straight until front measures same as Back to shoulder, ending at armhole edge.
Shape shoulder
Cast off.

sleeves

With 3.25mm needles, cast on 29 (31: 33: 35: 37: 39) sts.
K 5 rows.
Change to 4mm needles.
Moss st row (right side) P1, * k1, p1; rep from * to end.
This row **forms** the moss st and is repeated.
Work 3 more rows.
1st, 3rd 4th and 6th sizes only
Eyelet row Moss st 1 (–: 3: 1: –: 3), yrn, p2tog, * moss st 4, yrn, p2tog; rep from * to last 2 (–: 4: 2: –: 4) sts, moss st 2 (–: 4: 2: –: 4).
2nd and 5th sizes only
Eyelet row Moss st – (2: –: –: 2: –), yf, skpo, * moss st 4, yf, skpo; rep from * to last – (3: –: –: 3: –) sts, moss st – (3: –: –: 3: –).
All sizes
Cont in moss st and inc 1 st at each end of the next row and every foll 6th (6th: 6th: 6th: 6th: 8th) row until there are 37 (41: 45: 49: 53: 55) sts, taking all inc sts into moss st.
Cont straight until sleeve measures 13 (15: 17: 19: 22: 24)cm from cast-on edge, ending with a wrong side row.
Marking each end of last row with a coloured thread.
Work a further 6 rows.
Cast off.

collar

Join shoulder seams.
With right side facing and 3.25mm needles, slip 7 (7: 8: 8: 9: 9) sts from right front neck holder onto a needle, pick up and k13 (13: 15: 15: 17: 17) sts up right front neck, k29 (31: 31: 33: 33: 35) sts from back neck edge, pick up and k13 (13: 15: 15: 17: 17) sts down left front neck, moss st 2 (2: 3: 3: 4: 4) sts, then k5 from left front holder. **69 (71: 77: 79: 85: 87) sts.**
Cont in moss st with 5 sts in garter st for borders.
Next 2 rows Patt to last 20 sts, turn.
Next 2 rows Patt to last 16 sts, turn.
Next 2 rows Patt to last 12 sts, turn.
Next 2 rows Patt to last 8 sts, turn.
Next row (wrong side) Patt to end.
Cast off 3 sts at beg of next 2 rows. **63 (65: 71: 73: 79: 81) sts.**
Cont in moss st with 2 sts in garter st for borders.
Work straight for 4 (4: 4: 5: 5: 5)cm, ending with a wrong side row of collar.
Eyelet row (right side of collar) K2, moss st 2, yf, k2tog, patt to last 6 sts, k2tog, yf, moss st 2, k2.
Work 2 rows.
K 3 rows.
Cast off.

to make up

Using contrast colour work buttonhole st around every buttonhole and eyelet. Sew sleeves into armholes with row-ends above coloured threads sewn to sts cast-off at underarm. Join side and sleeve seams. Sew on buttons.

reversible hat

sizes
To fit ages 3–6 (9–12) months

materials
1 (2) x 50g balls Debbie Bliss Baby Cashmerino in each of lime (A) and grey (B)
Pair 3.25mm knitting needles

tension
26 sts and 34 rows to 10 cm square over 3 x 1 broken rib and 28 sts and 34 rows to 10 cm square over 1 x 1 broken rib both using 3.25mm needles.

abbreviations
See page 25.

inner/outer hat

With 3.25mm needles and A, cast on 98 (106) sts.
1st row (right side) * K3, p1; rep from * to last 2 sts, k2.
2nd row Purl.
Rep these 2 rows until hat measures 14 (15) cm, ending with a p row.
1st dec row (right side) * K3, p1, k1, k2tog, p1; rep from * to last 2 sts, k2. **86 (93) sts.**
Patt 3 rows as set.
2nd dec row * K1, k2tog, p1, k2, p1; rep from * to last 2 sts, k2. **74 (80) sts.**
Patt 3 rows as set.
3rd dec row * K2, p1, k2tog, p1; rep from * to last 2 sts, k2. **62 (67) sts.**
Patt 3 rows as set.
4th dec row * K2tog, p1, k1, p1; rep from * to last 2 sts, k2. **50 (54) sts.**
P 1 row.
5th dec row K1, * k2tog, p1, k1; rep from * to last st, k1. **38 (41) sts.**
P 1 row.
6th dec row * K2tog, p1; rep from * to last 2 sts, k2. **26 (28) sts.**
P 1 row.
7th dec row K1, * k2tog; rep from * to last st, k1. **14 (15) sts.**
P 1 row.
8th dec row K1, * k2tog; rep from * to last st, k1(0). **8 sts.**
Break yarn, thread through rem sts, pull up, secure and join seam.

outer/inner hat

With 3.25mm needles and B, cast on 104 (112) sts.
1st row (right side) * K1, p1; rep from * to end.
2nd row Purl.
Rep these 2 rows until hat measures 14 (15) cm, ending with a p row.
1st dec row (right side) * [K1, p1] twice, k1, k2tog, p1; rep from * to end. **91 (98) sts.**
Patt 3 rows.
2nd dec row * K1, k2tog, p1, k2, p1; rep from * to end. **78 (84) sts.**
Patt 3 rows.
3rd dec row * K2, p1, k2tog, p1; rep from * to end. **65 (70) sts.**
Patt 3 rows.
4th dec row * K2tog, p1, k1, p1; rep from * to end. **52 (56) sts.**
P 1 row.
5th dec row * K1, k2tog, p1; rep from * to end. **39 (42) sts.**
P 1 row.
6th dec row * K2tog, p1; rep from * to end. **26 (28) sts.**
P 1 row.
7th dec row K1, * k2tog; rep from * to last st, k1. **14 (15) sts.**
P 1 row.
8th dec row K0 (1), * k2tog; rep from * to end. **7 (8) sts.**
Break yarn, thread through rem sts, pull up, secure and join seam.

to make up

Turn inner/outer hat through to the wrong side, place this inside the outer/inner hat and slip stitch the hat pieces together all around the cast-on edges. Turn up the brim.

shawl collar sweater

measurements
To fit ages 3–6 (6–9: 9–12: 12–18: 18–24) months
finished measurements
Chest 50 (53: 60: 63: 70) cm
Length to shoulder 24 (26: 29: 32: 36) cm
Sleeve length (with cuff turned back) 14 (16: 18: 20: 22) cm

materials
3 (4: 5: 5: 6) x 50g balls Debbie Bliss Cashmerino Aran in stone
Pair each 4.50mm and 5mm knitting needles

tension
24 sts and 24 rows to 10 cm square over rib when slightly stretched using 5mm needles.

abbreviations
See page 25.

back
With 5mm needles, cast on 62 (66: 74: 78: 86) sts.
1st row (right side) K2, * p2, k2; rep from * to end.
2nd row P2, * k2, p2; rep from * to end.
These 2 rows **form** the rib.
Cont in rib until back measures 14 (15: 17: 18: 21) cm from cast-on edge, ending with a wrong-side row.
Shape armholes
Cast off 3 sts at beg of next 2 rows. **56 (60: 68: 72: 80) sts. ***
Cont in rib until back measures 24 (26: 29: 32: 36) cm from cast-on edge, ending with a wrong-side row.
Shape shoulders
Next row Cast off 17 (18: 21: 22: 25) sts, rib to last 17 (18: 21: 22: 25) sts and cast off these sts.
Leave rem 22 (24: 26: 28: 30) sts on a holder for collar.

front
Work as given for Back to **.
Shape neck
Next row Patt 21 (23: 27: 29: 33) sts, turn and work on these sts only for first side of neck shaping.
Work 1 row.
Dec 1 st at neck edge on next row and 3 (4: 5: 6: 7) foll 4th rows. **17 (18: 21: 22: 25) sts.**
Work straight until front measures same as Back to shoulder, ending with a wrong-side row.
Cast off.
With right side facing, rejoin yarn to rem sts, cast off 14 sts, patt to end.
Complete to match first side of neck shaping.

sleeves
With 5mm needles, cast on 42 (46: 50: 54: 58) sts.
1st row (right side) K2, * p2, k2; rep from * to end.
2nd row P2, * k2, p2; rep from * to end.
These 2 rows **form** the rib.

Work a further 6 rows in rib.
Change to 4.50mm needles.
Work a further 8 rows in rib.
Change to 5mm needles.
Cont in rib, inc 1 st at each end of the 5th row and every foll 4th row until there are 54 (60: 66: 74: 78) sts.
Cont straight until sleeve measures 19 (21: 23: 25: 27) cm from cast-on edge, ending with a wrong-side row.
Place markers at each end of last row.
Work a further 4 rows.
Cast off.

shawl collar   With right side facing and 4.50mm needles, rejoin yarn to 22 (24: 26: 28: 30) sts at back neck, cast on 4 (5: 4: 5: 4) sts, k2, p2, k0 (1: 0: 1: 0) across these sts, rib to end.
Next row (wrong side) Cast on 4 (5: 4: 5: 4) sts, p2, k2, p0 (1: 0: 1: 0) across these sts, rib to end.
Next row Cast on 4 sts, p2, k2, across these 4 sts, rib to end.
Next row Cast on 4 sts, k2, p2, across these 4 sts, rib to end.
Rep the last 2 rows 4 times more **70 (74: 74: 78: 78) sts.**
Rib a further 10 rows straight.
Change to 5mm needles.
Rib 2 rows.
Cast off loosely but evenly in rib.

to make up   Join shoulder seams. Sew sleeves into armholes with row ends above markers sewn to sts cast off at underarm. Join side and sleeve seams reversing seam for cuff. Sew cast-on edge of collar to neck edge, overlap right side of collar over left and sew row ends of collar to fronts.

smockcoat

measurements
To fit ages 3–6 (6–12: 12–18: 24–36) months
actual measurements
Chest 60 (64: 68: 71)cm
Length 36 (39: 43: 50)cm
Sleeve seam 16 (18: 20: 23)cm

materials
8 (8: 9: 10) x 50g balls Debbie Bliss Bella in chocolate
Pair each 3.25mm and 3.75mm knitting needles
4 (4: 4: 6) buttons
114cm of 15mm wide velvet ribbon

tension
22 sts and 36 rows to 10cm square over moss st on 3.75mm needles.

abbreviations
See page 25.

back

With 3.25mm needles, cast on 103 (109: 115: 121) sts.
K 3 rows.
Change to 3.75mm needles.
Next row P1, * k1, p1; rep from * to end.
This row forms the moss st.
Cont in moss st until back measures 21 (23: 26: 32)cm from cast-on edge, ending with a wrong side row.
Dec row Moss st 2, * work 3 tog, moss st 3; rep from * to last 5 sts, work 3 tog, moss st 2.
69 (73: 77: 81)sts
Change to 3.25mm needles.
Cont in moss st until back measures 26 (28: 31: 37)cm from cast-on edge, ending with a wrong side row.
Shape armholes
Cast off 5 (6: 7: 8) sts at beg of next 2 rows. **59 (61: 63: 65) sts.**
Cont straight until back measures 36 (39: 43: 50)cm from cast-on edge, ending with a wrong side row.
Shape shoulders
Cast off 10 sts at beg of next 2 rows and 10 (10: 10: 11) sts at beg of foll 2 rows.
Cast off rem 19 (21: 23: 23) sts.

left front

With 3.25mm needles, cast on 57 (59: 65: 67) sts.
K 3 rows.
Change to 3.75mm needles.
Next row (right side) * K1, p1; rep from * to last 3 sts, k3.
Next row K3, * p1, k1; rep from * to end.
These 2 rows set the moss st with garter st border.
Cont in patt until front measures 21 (23: 26: 32)cm from cast-on edge, ending with a wrong side row.
Dec row Moss st 3, [work 3 tog, moss st 3] 6 (6: 7: 7) times, moss st to last 3 sts, k3.
45 (47: 51: 53) sts.
Change to 3.25mm needles.
Cont in moss st until front measures 26 (28: 31: 37)cm from cast-on edge, ending with a wrong side row.
Shape armhole
Cast off 5 (6: 7: 8) sts at beg of next row. **40 (41: 44: 45) sts.**
Cont straight until front measures 27 (29: 33: 40)cm from cast-on edge, ending with a wrong side row.
Shape neck
Next row (right side) Moss st to last 3 sts, turn and leave these 3 sts on a safety pin for left collar.
Dec 1 st at neck edge on every row until 20 (20: 20: 21) sts rem.
Cont straight until front measures same as Back to shoulder, ending at side edge.
Shape shoulder
Cast off 10 sts at beg of next row.
Work 1 row.
Cast off rem 10 (10: 10: 11) sts.
Mark positions for buttons, the first pair level with first row of moss st yoke, the 2nd (2nd: 2nd: 3rd) pair 1cm below neck shaping and the remaining 0 (0: 0: 1) pair spaced evenly between.

right front

With 3.25mm needles, cast on 57 (59: 65: 67) sts.
K 3 rows.
Change to 3.75mm needles.
Next row (right side) K3, * p1, k1; rep from * to end.
Next row * K1, p1; rep from * to last 3 sts, k3.
These 2 rows **set** the moss st with garter st border.
Cont in patt until front measures 21 (23: 26: 32)cm from cast-on edge, ending with a wrong side row.
Change to 3.25mm needles.
Next row K3, yf, work 2 tog, moss 10 (12: 12: 14), work 2 tog, yf, moss st 2, turn and cont on these 19 (21: 21: 23) sts only.
Work a further 6 rows (for vertical slot) on these sts.
Leave these sts on a spare needle.
With right side facing, rejoin yarn to rem 38 (38: 44: 44) sts and work as follows:
Next row [Work 3 tog, moss st 3] 6 (6: 7: 7) times, moss st 2. **26 (26: 30: 30) sts.**
Work a further 6 rows in moss st on these sts.
Next row (wrong side) Moss to end, then moss st across sts on spare needle. **45 (47: 51: 53) sts.**
Cont as follows working 1 (1: 1: 2) more pairs of buttonholes to match markers.
Cont in moss st until front measures 26 (28: 31: 37)cm from cast-on edge, ending with a right side row.
Shape armhole
Cast off 5 (6: 7: 8) sts at beg of next row. **40 (41: 44: 45) sts.**
Cont straight until front measures 27 (29: 33: 40)cm from cast on edge, ending with a wrong side row.
Shape neck
Next row (right side) K3, leave these sts on a safety pin for right collar, moss st to end.
Dec 1 st at neck edge on every row until 20 (20: 20: 21) sts rem.
Cont straight until front measures same as Back to shoulder, ending at side edge.
Shape shoulder
Cast off 10 sts at beg of next row.
Work 1 row.
Cast off rem 10 (10: 10: 11) sts.

sleeves

With 3.25mm needles, cast on 31 (33: 37: 39) sts.
K 3 rows.
Change to 3.75mm needles.
Next row P1, * k1, p1; rep from * to end.
This row **forms** the moss st.
Work 3 more rows.
Inc 1 st at each end of the next row and every foll 6th row until there are 41 (47: 55: 59) sts.
Cont straight until sleeve measures 16 (18: 20: 23)cm from cast-on edge, ending with a wrong side row.
Mark each end of last row with a coloured thread.
Work a further 8 (10: 10: 12) rows.
Cast off.

left collar

With right side facing and 3.25mm needles, k across 3 sts of left front band.
K 1 row.
Cont in garter st and inc 1 st at each end of the next row and every foll 4th row until there are 21 sts, ending at outer edge of collar.
Shape collar
** Next 2 rows K12, sl 1, turn, k to end.
K 4 rows.**
Rep from ** to ** until short edge of collar fits up left side of front neck and halfway across back neck edge.
Cast off.

right collar

With wrong side facing and 3.25mm needles, k across 3 sts on right front band.
Cont in garter st and inc 1 st at each end of the next row and every foll 4th row until there are 21 sts.
K 1 row, so ending at outer edge of collar.
Shape collar
** Next 2 rows K12, sl 1, turn k to end.
K 4 rows.**
Rep from ** to ** until short edge of collar fits up right front neck and halfway across back neck edge.
Cast off.

to make up

Join shoulder seams. Join cast-off edges of collar. Sew collar in place. Sew sleeves into armholes with row-ends above markers sewn to sts cast off at underarm. Join side and sleeve seams. Sew on buttons. Cut ribbon in half and sew one piece to left front edge, level with vertical slot on right front and rem piece sewn to right front edge to match.

buggy blanket

size
Approximately 45 x 71 cm

materials
2 x 50g balls Debbie Bliss Cashmerino Aran each in pale blue (A) and lilac (C), and 1 x 50g ball each in mid blue (B), pale green (D) and mid green (E)
Pair 5mm knitting needles or 5mm circular knitting needle

tension
18 sts and 24 rows to 10cm over st st using 5mm needles.

abbreviations
See page 25.

note
Use the Intarsia method (see page 30), knitting with separate small balls of yarn for each area of colour and twisting yarns on wrong side when changing colour to avoid holes.

front

With 5mm needles and A, cast on 83 sts.
1st row K1, * p1, k1; rep from * to end.
Rep the last row 3 times more.
1st line
Next row (right side) With A [k1, p1] twice, k15 E, k15 D, k15 C, k15 B, k15 A, with A [p1, k1] twice.
Next row With A [k1, p1] twice, p15 A, p15 B, p15 C, p15 D, p15 E, with A [p1, k1] twice.
These 2 rows **set** the position of the 1st line of st st squares (with 4 moss sts in A at each side) and are repeated.
Work a further 18 rows.

2nd line

Next row (right side) With A [k1, p1] twice, k15 B, k15 A, k15 E, k15 D, k15 C, with A [p1, k1] twice.
Next row With A [k1, p1] twice, p15 C, p15 D, p15 E, p15 A, p15 B, with A [p1, k1] twice.
These 2 rows **set** the position of the 2nd line of st st squares (with 4 moss sts in A at each side)
and are repeated.
Work a further 18 rows.

3rd line

Next row (right side) With A [k1, p1] twice, k15 C, k15 D, k15 B, k15 A, k15 E, with A [p1, k1] twice.
Next row With A [k1, p1] twice, p15 E, p15 A, p15 B, p15 D, p15 C, with A [p1, k1] twice.
These 2 rows **set** the position of the 3rd line of st st squares (with 4 moss sts in A at each side)
and are repeated.
Work a further 18 rows.

4th line

Next row (right side) With A [k1, p1] twice, k15 A, k15 E, k15 C, k15 D, k15 B, with A [p1, k1] twice.
Next row With A [k1, p1] twice, p15 B, p15 D, p15 C, p15 E, p15 A, with A [p1, k1] twice.
These 2 rows **set** the position of the 4th line of st st squares (with 4 moss sts in A at each side)
and are repeated.
Work a further 18 rows.

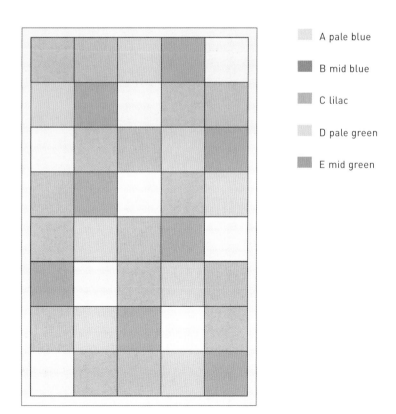

A pale blue

B mid blue

C lilac

D pale green

E mid green

5th line

Next row (right side) With A [k1, p1] twice, k15 D, k15 B, k15 A, k15 E, k15 C, with A [p1, k1] twice.

Next row With A [k1, p1] twice, p15 C, p15 E, p15 A, p15 B, p15 D, with A [p1, k1] twice.

These 2 rows **set** the position of the 5th line of st st squares (with 4 moss sts in A at each side) and are repeated.

Work a further 18 rows.

6th line

Next row (right side) With A [k1, p1] twice, k15 E, k15 D, k15 C, k15 B, k15 A, with A [p1, k1] twice.

Next row With A [k1, p1] twice, p15 A, p15 B, p15 C, p15 D, p15 E, with A [p1, k1] twice.

These 2 rows **set** the position of the 6th line of st st squares (with 4 moss sts in A at each side) and are repeated.

Work a further 18 rows.

7th line

Next row (right side) With A [k1, p1] twice, k15 C, k15 B, k15 A, k15 E, k15 D, with A [p1, k1] twice.

Next row With A [k1, p1] twice, p15 D, p15 E, p15 A, p15 B, p15 C, with A [p1, k1] twice.

These 2 rows **set** the position of the 7th line of st st squares (with 4 moss sts in A at each side) and are repeated.

Work a further 18 rows.

8th line

Next row (right side) With A [k1, p1] twice, k15 A, k15 E, k15 D, k15 C, k15 B, with A [p1, k1] twice.

Next row With A [k1, p1] twice, p15 A, p15 B, p15 C, p15 D, p15 E, with A [p1, k1] twice.

These 2 rows **set** the position of the 8th line of st st squares (with 4 moss sts in A at each side) and are repeated.

Work a further 18 rows.

Next row (right side) With A [k1, p1] twice, k75 A, with A [p1, k1] twice.

Next row With A, k1, * p1, k1; rep from * to end.

Rep the last row 3 times more.

Cast off in moss st.

back

With 5mm needles and A, cast on 83 sts.

1st row K1, * p1, k1; rep from * to end.

Rep the last row 3 times more.

Next row (right side) With A [k1, p1] twice, k75 E, with A [p1, k1] twice.

Next row With A [k1, p1] twice, p75 E, with A [p1, k1] twice.

These 2 rows **form** the st st with moss st edges in A and are repeated, working stripes as follows:

Keeping the moss st edges in A throughout, work a further 18 rows in E, then work in 20 row stripes of C, A, D, B, C, D, E, ending with a wrong-side row.

Next row (right side) With A [k1, p1] twice, k75 A, with A [p1, k1] twice.

Next row With A, k1, * p1, k1; rep from * to end.

Rep the last row 3 times more.

Cast off in moss st.

to make up

Join Back to Front around edges.

striped sweater

measurements

To fit ages 3–6 (6–9: 9–12) months

actual measurements

Chest 50 (53: 59)cm

Length to shoulder 24 (26: 28)cm

Sleeve length 16 (18: 20)cm

materials

2 (3: 3) x 50g balls Debbie Bliss Bella in green (A) and 2 (2: 3) x 50g balls in ecru (B)

Pair each 3.25mm and 3.75mm knitting needles

6 small buttons

tension

22 sts and 30 rows to 10cm square over st st using 3.75mm needles

abbreviations

See page 25.

front

With 3.25mm needles and A, cast on 57 (61: 67) sts.

K 5 rows.

Change to 3.75mm needles.

Next row (right side) K4A, k49 (53: 59)B, k4A.

Next row K4A, p49 (53: 59)B, k4A.

Next row K all sts in A.

Next row K4A, p49 (53: 59)A, k4A.

Next row K4A, k49 (53: 59)B, k4A.

Next row (wrong side) P all sts in B.

Beg with a k row, work in st st in stripe sequence of 2 rows A and 2 rows B.

Cont until work measures 21 (23: 25)cm from cast-on edge, ending with a wrong side row.

Keeping the stripe sequence correct, work as follows:

Shape neck

Next row (right side) K17 (18: 20), turn and cont on these sts only for first side of neck.

Work 2cm in stripes, ending with a wrong side row.

Buttonhole shoulder band

Change to 3.25mm needles and A.

K 2 rows.

Buttonhole row (right side) K4 (5: 5), yf, k2tog, k5 (5: 6), yf, k2tog, k4 (4: 5).

K 2 rows.

Cast off knitwise.

With right side facing, slip 23 (25: 27) sts at centre front onto a holder, rejoin correct yarn, and knit to end.

Complete to match first side, working buttonhole row as follows:

Buttonhole row (right side) K4 (4: 5), k2tog, yf, k5 (5: 6), k2tog, yf, k4 (5: 5).

back

Work as given for Front, omitting buttonholes on shoulder bands.

sleeves

With 3.25mm needles and A, cast on 35 (37: 39) sts.

K 5 rows.

Change to 3.75mm needles.

Beg with a k row in B, work in st st in stripe sequence as follows:

2 rows B.

2 rows A.

But **at the same time**, inc 1 st at each end of the 7th row and every foll 8th row until there are 43 (47: 51) sts.

Cont straight until sleeve measures 16 (18: 20)cm from cast-on edge, ending with a right side row.

Cast off.

neckband

With right side facing, 3.25mm needles and A, pick up and k 8 sts down left front neck, k across 23 (25: 27) sts at centre front, pick up and k 8 sts up right front neck. **39 (41: 43) sts.**

K 1 row.

Buttonhole row K2, yf, k2tog, k2, skpo, k2tog, k19 (21: 23), skpo, k2tog, k3, yf, k2tog, k1.

K 1 row.

Next row K5, skpo, k2tog, k17 (19: 21), skpo, k2tog, k5.

Cast off knitwise, dec at corners as before.

Work back neckband in the same way, omitting buttonholes but working corner decreases.

to make up

Lap buttonhole band over button band at shoulders and catch stitch together at side edges.

Matching centre of cast-off edge of sleeve to centre of shoulder bands, sew on sleeves.

Starting at top side of side splits, join side seams. Then join sleeve seams. Sew on buttons.

measurements
To fit ages 0–3 (3–6) months
finished measurements
Length to shoulder 55 (60) cm

materials
8 (9) x 50g balls Debbie Bliss Cashmerino Aran in ecru
Pair 4.50mm knitting needles
4.50mm circular knitting needle
40 cm zip fastener

tension
20 rows and 42 rows to 10 cm square over garter st using 4^{1}/$_{2}$mm needles.

abbreviations
kfb = knit into front and back of next st.
See page 25.

hooded carrying bag

**back, front
and sleeves**
(worked in one piece)

With 4.50mm needles, cast on 54 (62) sts.
1st row Knit.
This row **forms** garter st and is repeated.
Cont straight until back measures 46 (48) cm from cast-on edge, ending with a wrong-side row.
Change to 4.50mm circular needle.
Shape sleeves
Cast on 30 (36) sts at beg of next 2 rows. **114 (134) sts.**
Cont straight in garter st until back measures 55 (60) cm from cast-on edge, ending with a wrong-side row.
Place a marker at each end of last row for shoulder line.
Divide for fronts
Next row (right side) With 4.50mm needles, k43 (53), turn and cont on these sts only for right front, leaving rem sts on the circular needle.
Shape neck
Next row (wrong side) Kfb, k to end. **44 (54) sts.**
K 1 row.
Rep the last 2 rows once more. **45 (55) sts.**
Next row Cast on 2 sts, k to end. **47 (57) sts.**
K 1 row.
Next row Cast on 3 sts, k to end. **50 (60) sts.**

K 1 row.

Rep the last 2 rows once more. **53 (63) sts.**

Next row Cast on 7 sts, k to end. **60 (70) sts.**

Mark front edge of last row with a coloured thread.

Cont straight in garter st until work measures 10 (12) cm from shoulder line marker, ending with a wrong-side row.

Shape sleeve

Next row (right side) Cast off 30 (36) sts, k to end. **30 (34) sts.**

Cont in garter st until work measures 40 cm from front edge marker, ending with a right-side row.

Next row Cast off 3 sts, slip rem 27 (31) sts onto a holder.

Return to sts on circular needle and with right side facing, slip 28 sts at centre back neck onto a holder, rejoin yarn to rem 43 (53) sts for left front, k to end.

K 1 row.

Next row (right side) Kfb, k to end. **44 (54) sts.**

K 1 row.

Rep the last 2 rows once more. **45 (55) sts.**

Next row Cast on 2 sts, k to end. **47 (57) sts.**

K 1 row.

Next row Cast on 3 sts, k to end. **50 (60) sts.**

K 1 row.

Rep the last 2 rows once more. **53 (63) sts.**

K 1 row.

Next row Cast on 4 sts, k to end. **57 (67) sts.**

Mark front edge of last row with a coloured thread.

Cont straight in garter st until work measures 10 (12) cm from shoulder line marker, ending with a right-side row.

Shape sleeve

Next row (wrong side) Cast off 30 (36) sts, k to end. **27 (31) sts.**

Cont in garter st until work measures 40 cm from front edge marker, ending with a right-side row.

Next row (wrong side) K 27 (31) sts of left front, then k across 27 (31) sts on right front holder. **54 (62) sts.**

Cont straight until front measures 55 (60) cm from shoulder line, ending with a right-side row.

Cast off.

hood

With right side facing and 4.50mm needles, pick up and k22 sts up right front neck to shoulder, then work k2, [m1, k2] 13 times across 28 sts on back neck holder, then pick up and k20 sts down left front neck. **83 sts.**

Work in garter st until hood measures 20 cm from pick-up row.

Cast off.

to make up

Fold cast-off edge of hood in half and stitch to form top seam. Fold along shoulder line and stitch front to back along sleeve seams and around side and lower edges. Handstitch zip in place with left front edge sewn close to the zip teeth and right front, sewn approximately 1 cm from the edge, so forming a fly front. Catchstitch cast-off sts of lower end of fly front in place.

measurements

To fit ages 0–3 (3-6: 6–9: 9–12: 12–24) months

materials

1 x 50g ball Debbie Bliss Baby Cashmerino in each of grape (M) and lavender (C)
Set of four double pointed knitting needles in each of 3.75mm and 3.25mm

tension

25 sts and 34 rows to 10cm square over st st using $3^1/_4$mm needles.

abbreviations

See page 25.

wee willie winkie hat 183

to make up

With a set of four 3.75mm double pointed needles (see page 41) and M, cast on 88 (96: 104: 112: 120) sts.

Arrange sts on 3 of 4 needles and place a marker after last st to indicate end of rounds.

Taking care not to twist the edge, work in rounds of k1, p1 rib for 2 (2: 3: 3: 3)cm.

Change to set of four 3.25mm needles and C and cont to work a further 1cm in rounds of rib.

Working in rounds of st st (k every round) and stripe patt of 2 rounds C, 2 rounds M throughout, cont straight until work measures 12 (12: 14: 14: 16)cm from cast-on edge.

Shape top

Dec round [K20 (22: 24: 26: 28), k2tog] 4 times. **84 (92: 100: 108: 116) sts.**

Work 2 rounds.

Dec round [K19 (21: 23: 25: 27), k2tog] 4 times. **80 (88: 96: 104: 112) sts.**

Work 2 rounds.

Dec round [K18 (20: 22: 24: 26), k2tog] 4 times. **76 (84: 92: 100: 108) sts.**

Work 2 rounds.

Cont in this way to dec 4 sts as set on next row and every 3rd round until 40 (44: 48: 52: 56) sts rem.

Work 1 round.

Cont to dec 4 sts as before on next round and every foll alt round until 8 sts rem.

Dec round [K2tog] 4 times. **4 sts.**

Break yarn, thread through rem sts, pull up and secure.

Make a pompon (see page 43) in M and sew to top of hat.

sizes
To fit ages 3–6 (6–12: 12–18) months

materials
1 x 50g ball Debbie Bliss Baby Cashmerino in each of main colour (M) and contrast colour (C)
Set of four double pointed 3.25mm knitting needles

tension
25 sts and 34 rows to 10cm square over st st using 3.25mm needles.

abbreviations
See page 25.

two tone socks 185

to make

With 3.25mm needles and C, cast on 32 (36: 40) sts.
Arrange these sts on 3 needles and cont in rounds.
Rib round * K1, p1; rep from * to end.
Rib a further 3 (5: 7) rounds.
Change to M.
Now work in rounds of k, so forming st st.
K 2 (2: 4) rounds.
Dec round K5, k2tog, k to last 7 sts, skpo, k5. 30 (34: 38) sts.
K 3 (5: 7) rounds.
Dec round K4, k2tog, k to last 6 sts, skpo, k4. 28 (32: 36) sts.
Work 3 (5: 7) rounds.
Dec round K3, k2tog, k5 (6: 7), k2tog, [k5 (6: 7), skpo] twice, k2 (3: 4). **24 (28: 32) sts.**
Cut off M.
Divide sts onto 3 needles as follows: slip first 7 (8: 9) sts onto first needle,
next 5 (6: 7) sts onto second needle and next 5 (6: 7) sts onto 3rd needle, then slip
last 7 (8: 9) sts onto other end of first needle.

Shape heel

With right side facing, join C to 14 (16: 18) sts on first needle.

Cont in st st rows on these 14 (16: 18) sts only.

Beg with a k row, work 10 rows st st.

Next row K9 (11: 13), skpo, turn.

Next row Sl 1, p4 (6: 8), p2tog, turn.

Next row Sl 1, k4 (6: 8), skpo, turn.

Next row Sl 1, p4 (6: 8), p2tog, turn.

Rep the last 2 rows twice more. **6 (8: 10) sts.**

Break off yarn.

Reset sts on 3 needles as follows: slip first 3(4:5) sts of heel sts onto a safety pin, place marker here to indicate beg of round. Join M to rem sts, with first needle k3(4:5), then pick up and k8 sts along side of heel, with second needle k10(12:14), with 3rd needle pick up and k8 sts along other side of heel, k3(4:5) from safety pin. **32 (36: 40) sts.**

Cont in rounds.

K 1 round.

Dec round K9 (10: 11), k2tog, k10 (12: 14), k2tog tbl, k9 (10: 11). **30 (34: 38) sts.**

K 1 round.

Dec round K8 (9: 10), k2tog, k10 (12: 14), k2tog tbl, k8 (9: 10). **28 (32: 36) sts.**

K 1 round.

Dec round K7 (8: 9), k2tog, k10 (12: 14), k2tog tbl, k7 (8: 9). **26 (30: 34) sts.**

K 1 round.

Dec round K6 (7: 8), k2tog, k10 (12: 14), k2tog tbl, k6 (7: 8). **24 (28: 32) sts.**

Work 11 (13: 17) rounds straight.

Shape toe

Dec round [K2tog tbl, k4 (5: 6)] 4 times. **20 (24: 28) sts.**

K 1 round.

Dec round [K2tog tbl, k3 (4: 5)] 4 times. **16 (20: 24) sts.**

K 1 round.

Change to C.

Dec round [K2tog tbl, k2 (3: 4)] 4 times. **12 (16: 20) sts.**

K 1 round.

2nd and 3rd sizes only

Dec round [K2tog tbl, k-(2: 3)] 4 times. **- (12: 16) sts.**

3rd size only

K 1 round.

Dec round [K2tog tbl, k-(-: 2)] 4 times. **– (-: 12) sts.**

K 1 round.

All sizes

Dec round [K2tog tbl] 6 times.

Break off yarn, thread through rem 6 sts, pull up and secure.

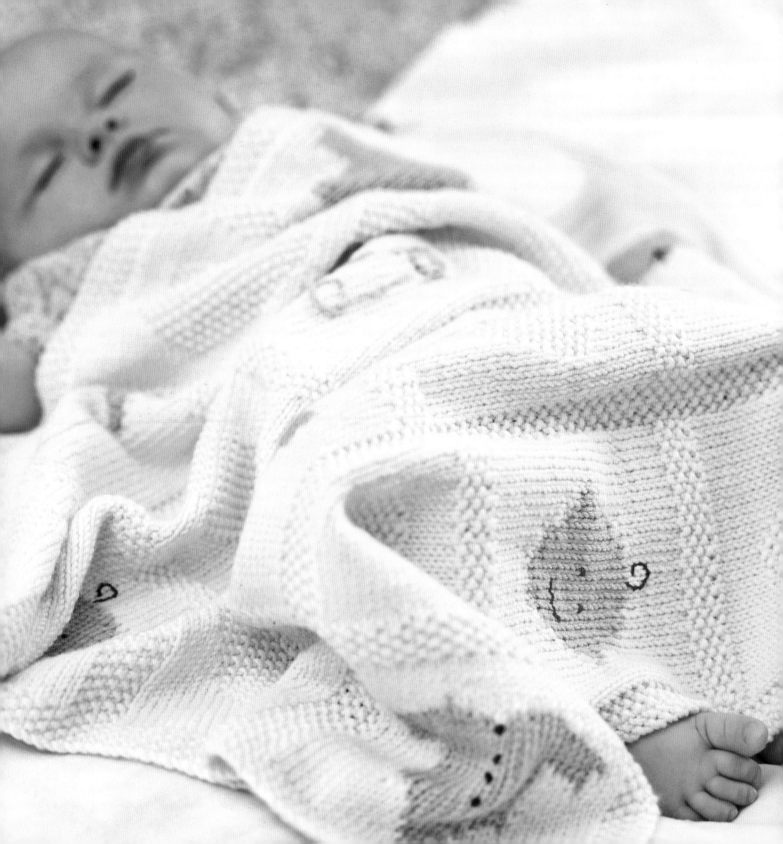

baby blanket

measurements
Length 60cm
Width 54cm

materials
4 x 50g balls Debbie Bliss Baby Cashmerino in ecru (M) and 1 x 50g ball each in
pale pink (A) and pale blue (B)
Long circular or pair long 3.25mm knitting needles
Brown stranded cotton
Pale pink sewing thread

tension
25 sts and 34 rows to 10cm square over st st using 3.25mm needles.

abbreviations
See page 25.

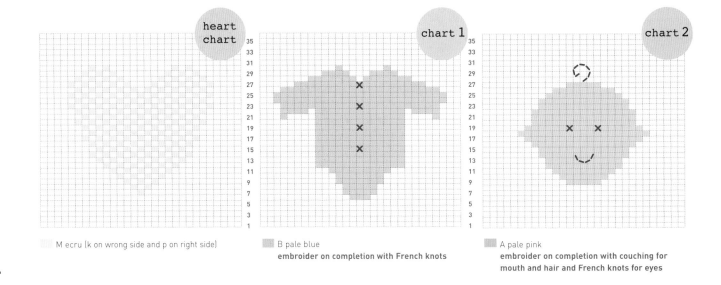

M ecru (k on wrong side and p on right side)

B pale blue
embroider on completion with French knots

A pale pink
**embroider on completion with couching for
mouth and hair and French knots for eyes**

chart notes

All charts are worked in st st unless otherwise indicated. When working from a chart, odd rows
are k rows and are read from right to left, even rows are p rows and read from left to right. When
working motifs, use the Intarsia method (see page 30), knitting with separate small balls of yarn
for each area of colour and twisting yarns on wrong side when changing colour to avoid holes.

blanket

With 3.25mm needles and M, cast on 141 sts.
Moss st row K1, [p1, k1] to end.
Rep this row 5 times more.

First line of motifs

Next row (right side) Moss st 5, work across 29 sts of Chart 1, moss st 5, work across 29 sts of
Heart Chart, moss st 5, work across 29 sts of Chart 2, moss st 5, work across 29 sts of Heart
Chart, moss st 5.
Cont as set on last row for moss st and charts until all 36 rows of charts have been worked.
Work 6 rows in moss st across all sts.

Second line of motifs

Next row (right side) Moss st 5, work across 29 sts of Heart Chart, moss st 5, work across 29 sts
of Chart 3, moss st 5, work across 29 sts of Heart Chart, moss st 5, work across 29 sts of Chart 4,
moss st 5.
Cont as set on last row until all 36 rows of charts have been worked.
Work 6 rows in moss st across all sts.

Third line of motifs

Next row (right side) Moss st 5, work across 29 sts of Chart 2, moss st 5, work across 29 sts of

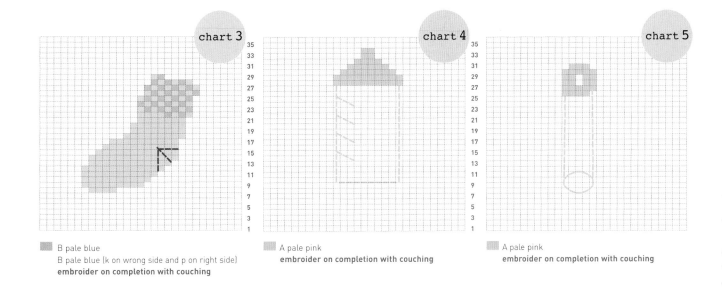

chart 3

35 33 31 29 27 25 23 21 19 17 15 13 11 9 7 5 3 1

B pale blue
B pale blue (k on wrong side and p on right side)
embroider on completion with couching

chart 4

35 33 31 29 27 25 23 21 19 17 15 13 11 9 7 5 3 1

A pale pink
embroider on completion with couching

chart 5

35 33 31 29 27 25 23 21 19 17 15 13 11 9 7 5 3 1

A pale pink
embroider on completion with couching

baby blanket

191

Heart Chart, moss st 5, work across 29 sts of Chart 5, moss st 5, work across 29 sts of Heart Chart, moss st 5.

Cont as set on last row until all 36 rows of charts have been worked.

Work 6 rows in moss st across all sts.

Fourth line of motifs

Next row (right side) Moss st 5, work across 29 sts of Heart Chart, moss st 5, work across 29 sts of Chart 4, moss st 5, work across 29 sts of Heart Chart, moss st 5, work across 29 sts of Chart 1, moss st 5.

Cont as set on last row until all 36 rows of charts have been worked.

Work 6 rows in moss st across all sts.

Fifth line of motifs

Next row (right side) Moss st 5, work across 29 sts of Chart 5, moss st 5, work across 29 sts of Heart Chart, moss st 5, work across 29 sts of Chart 3, moss st 5, work across 29 sts of Heart Chart, moss st 5.

Cont as set on last row until all 36 rows of charts have been worked.

Work 5 rows in moss st across all sts.

Cast off in moss st.

to make up

Work embroidery as indicated on charts (see above). For the French knots and couched lines on Charts 1, 2, and 3, use three strands of brown stranded cotton, and use one strand for couching threads in place. For the couched lines on charts 4 and 5, use one strand of pale pink yarn (A), and couch in place with sewing thread.

measurements

To fit ages 3–6 (6–9: 9–12: 12–18: 18–24) months

actual measurements

Chest 47 (52: 56: 61: 66)cm

Length to shoulder 22 (24: 26: 28: 32)cm

Sleeve length 13 (15: 17: 19: 22)cm

materials

2 (3: 3: 3: 4) x 50g balls of Debbie Bliss Baby Cashmerino in teal (M)

1 x 50g ball each pale blue (A), indigo (B), lime (C), burgundy (D) and ecru (E)

Pair each 2.75mm, 3mm and 3.25mm knitting needles

One each 2.75mm, 3mm and 3.25mm circular needles

6 (6: 6: 7: 7) buttons

tension

25 sts and 34 rows to 10cm square over st st using 3.25mm needles.

abbreviations

See page 25.

fairislecardigan

back

With 3mm needles and A, cast on 61 (67: 73: 79: 85) sts.

1st rib row K1, * p1, k1; rep from * to end.

Change to M.

2nd rib row P1, * k1, p1; rep from * to end.

Rep the 2 rib rows 2 (2: 3: 3: 4) times more.

Change to 3.25mm needles.

Beg with a k row, work in st st until back measures 12 (13: 14: 15: 17)cm from cast-on edge, ending with a p row.

Shape armholes

Cast off 4 sts at beg of next 2 rows. **53 (59: 65: 71: 77) sts.**

Cont straight until back measures 14 (16: 18: 20: 24)cm from cast-on edge, ending with a p row.

Shape yoke

Next row (right side) K22 (24: 26: 28: 30), turn and work on these sts.

Cast off 3 (4: 5: 6: 7) sts at beg of next row, and 2 sts at beg of 3 foll alt rows.

Now dec 1 st on every foll alt row until 6 (7: 8: 9: 10) sts rem.

Cont straight until back measures 22 (24: 26: 28: 32)cm from cast-on edge, ending at armhole edge.

Shape shoulder

Cast off.

With right side facing, slip centre 9 (11: 13: 15: 17) sts onto a holder, rejoin yarn to rem sts, k to end.
P 1 row.
Complete to match first side.

left front

With 3mm needles and A, cast on 29 (33: 35: 37: 41) sts.
1st rib row P1, * k1, p1; rep from * to end.
Change to M.
2nd rib row K1, * p1, k1; rep from * to end.
Rep the 2 rib rows 2 (2: 3: 3: 4) times more.
Change to 3.25mm needles.
Beg with a k row, work in st st until front measures 12 (13: 14: 15: 17)cm from cast-on edge, ending with a p row.
Shape armhole
Cast off 4 sts at beg of next row. **25 (29: 31: 33: 37) sts.**
Cont straight until front measures 14 (16: 18: 20: 24)cm from cast-on edge, ending with a p row.
Shape yoke
Next row (right side) K22 (24: 26: 28: 30), turn and work on these sts, leave rem 3 (5: 5: 5: 7) sts on a holder.
Cast off 3 (4: 5: 6: 7) sts at beg of next row, and 2 sts at beg of 3 foll alt rows.
Now dec 1 st at beg of every foll alt row until 6 (7: 8: 9: 10) sts rem.
Cont straight until front measures 22 (24: 26: 28: 32)cm from cast-on edge, ending at armhole edge.
Shape shoulder
Cast off.

right front

With 3mm needles and A, cast on 29 (33: 35: 37: 41) sts.
1st rib row P1, * k1, p1; rep from * to end.
Change to M.
2nd rib row K1, * p1, k1; rep from * to end.
Rep the 2 rib rows 2 (2: 3: 3: 4) times more.
Change to 3.25mm needles.
Beg with a k row, work in st st until front measures 12 (13: 14: 15: 17)cm from cast-on edge, ending with a k row.
Shape armhole
Cast off 4 sts at beg of next row. **25 (29: 31: 33: 37) sts.**
Cont straight until front measures 14 (16: 18: 20: 24)cm from cast-on edge, ending with a p row.
Shape yoke
Next row (right side) K3 (5: 5: 5: 7) sts, leave these sts on a holder, k to end. **22 (24: 26: 28: 30) sts.**
P 1 row.
Cast off 3 (4: 5: 6: 7) sts at beg of next row, and 2 sts at beg of 3 foll alt rows.
Now dec 1 st at beg of every foll alt row until 6 (7: 8: 9: 10) sts rem.
Cont straight until front measures 22 (24: 26: 28: 32)cm from cast-on edge, ending at armhole edge.
Shape shoulder
Cast off.

chart notes

When working yoke from 4th–18th rows of chart, work 1 edge st at beg of right side and end of wrong side rows, repeat the 12 st patt across row, then work 2 edge sts at beg of wrong side and end of right side rows. Strand and weave in yarn not in use across wrong side of work.

— 12 st patt repeat —

■ M teal ■ A pale blue ■ B indigo ■ C lime ■ D burgundy ▨ E ecru

196

sleeves

With 3mm needles and B, cast on 32 (34: 38: 42: 46) sts.
Rib row * K1, p1; rep from * to end.
This row **forms** the rib.
Change to M.
Rep the rib row 5 (5: 7: 7: 9) times more.
Change to 3.25mm needles.
Beg with a k row, work in st st and inc 1 st at each end of the next (3rd: 5th: 3rd: 3rd) row and every foll 4th row until there are 50 (54: 58: 66: 74) sts.
Cont straight until sleeve measures 13 (15: 17: 19: 22)cm from cast-on edge, ending with a p row.
Mark each end of last row with a coloured thread.
Work a further 4 rows.
Cast off.

yoke

Join shoulder seams.
With right side facing, 3.25mm circular needle and M, slip 3 (5: 5: 5: 7) sts from right front holder onto a needle, pick up and k9 (10: 11: 12: 13) sts from cast-off sts, 13 (14: 15: 16: 17) sts to shoulder, 13 (14: 15: 16: 17) sts along row ends from shoulder to start of cast-off sts, 9 (10: 11: 12: 13) sts from cast-off sts, k9 (11: 13: 15: 17) sts from centre back holder, pick up and k9 (10: 11: 12: 13) sts from cast-off sts, 13 (14: 15: 16: 17) sts to shoulder, 13 (14: 15: 16: 17) sts along row ends from shoulder to start of cast-off sts, 9 (10: 11: 12: 13) sts from cast-off sts, then k3 (5: 5: 5: 7) sts from left front holder. **103 (117: 127: 137: 151) sts.**
Next row (wrong side) P to end.

Next row (1st row of Chart) (right side) K1B, * 1E, 1B; rep from * to end.

Next row (2nd row of Chart) P1E, * 1D, 1E; rep from * to end.

Dec row (3rd row of Chart) (right side) With M, k5 (7: 3: 3: 7), [k4 (4: 6: 8: 7), k2tog] 15 (17: 15: 13: 15) times, k2tog, k6 (6: 2: 2: 7). **87 (99: 111: 123: 135) sts.**

Work 4th to 10th row from Chart.

Change to 3mm circular needle.

Work 11th to 18th row from Chart.

Dec row (19th row of Chart) (right side) With M, k3, * k2tog, k5, k2tog, k3; rep from * to end. **73 (83: 93: 103: 113) sts.**

Work 2nd then 1st rows from Chart as before.

Cont in M only.

P 1 row.

K 1 row.

Dec row (wrong side) P3 * p2tog, p3; rep from * to end. **59 (67: 75: 83: 91) sts.**

K 1 row.

P 1 row.

Change to 2.75mm needles.

1st rib row K1, * p1, k1; rep from * to end.

2nd rib row P1, * k1, p1; rep from * to end.

3rd rib row K1, * p1, k1; rep from * to end.

Change to A.

4th rib row P1, * k1, p1; rep from * to end.

Cast off in rib.

button band

With right side facing, 2.75mm needles and M, pick up and k55 (61: 67: 75: 91) sts along left front edge.

Work 3 rows in rib as given for Back.

Change to B.

Rib 1 row.

Cast off in rib.

buttonhole band

With right side facing, 2.75mm needles and M, pick up and k55 (61: 67: 75: 91) sts along right front edge.

Work 1 row in rib as given for Back.

Buttonhole row (right side) Rib 2 (2: 2: 3: 2), [rib 2tog, yf, rib 8 (9: 10: 9: 12) sts] 5 (5: 5: 6: 6) times, rib 2tog, yf, rib 1 (2: 3: 4: 3).

Rib 1 row.

Change to B.

Rib 1 row.

Cast off in rib.

to make up

Sew sleeves into armholes with row ends above markers sewn to sts cast off at underarm. Join side and sleeve seams. Sew on buttons.

measurements

To fit ages 3–6 (6–9) months
finished measurements
Over nappy 51 (56) cm
Length 22 (24) cm

materials

2 (2) x 50g balls Debbie Bliss Baby Cashmerino in grey
Pair each 2.75mm and 3.25mm knitting needles
Waist length of 2cm wide elastic

tension

25 sts and 34 rows to 10 cm square over st st using 3.25mm needles.

abbreviations

See page 25.

baby knickers

back

With 2.75mm needles, cast on 66 (76) sts.
Rib row * K1, p1; rep from * to end.
Rib a further 9 rows.
Change to 3.25mm needles.
Back shaping
Next 2 rows K to last 30 sts, turn, sl 1, p to last 30 sts, turn.
Next 2 rows Sl 1, k to last 24 sts, turn, sl 1, p to last 24 sts, turn.
Next 2 rows Sl 1, k to last 18 sts, turn, sl 1, p to last 18 sts, turn.
Next 2 rows Sl 1, k to last 12 sts, turn, sl 1, p to last 12 sts, turn.
Next 2 rows Sl 1, k to last 6 sts, turn, sl 1, p to last 6 sts, turn.
Next row Sl 1, k to end.
Inc row P3, m1, [p6, m1] 4 times, p12 (22), [m1, p6] 4 times, m1, p3. **76 (86) sts.**
Beg with a k row, cont in st st.
Work 42 (52) rows.
Dec 1 st at each end of the next row and 9 (7) foll alt rows. **56 (70) sts.**
P 1 row.
Dec 1 st at each end of the next 16 (20) rows. **24 (30) sts.**
Work 20 (22) rows without shaping.
Break off yarn and leave these sts on a holder.

Side of right leg
With 3.25mm needles, cast on 2 sts.
P 1 row.
Next row K1, m1, k1.
Next row P2, m1, p1.
Next row K1, m1, k to end.
Next row P to last st, m1, p1.
Rep the last 2 rows 10 (11) times. **26 (28) sts.**
Break off yarn and leave these sts on a holder.
Side of left leg
With 3.25mm needles, cast on 2 sts.
P 1 row.
Next row K1, m1, k1.
Next row P1, m1, p2.
Next row K to last st, m1, k1.
Next row P1, m1, p to end.
Rep the last 2 rows 10 (11) times. **26 (28) sts.**
Next row K these 26 (28) sts, k24 (30) sts from first holder, then k26 (28) sts from second holder.
76 (86) sts.
Work 18 (26) rows without shaping.
Dec row [P5, p2tog] 5 times, p6 (16), [p2tog, p5] 5 times. **66 (76) sts.**
Change to 2.75mm needles.
Rib row * K1, p1; rep from * to end.
Rib a further 9 rows.
Cast off in rib.

leg edgings
With right side facing and 3.25mm needles, pick up and k72 (78) sts evenly round leg opening.
Rib row * K1, p1; rep from * to end.
Rib 1 more row.
Change to 2.75mm needles.
Rib a further 3 rows.
Cast-off row Cast off 3 sts, * slip st back onto left-hand needle, cast on 2 sts, cast off 6 sts; rep from *, ending last rep cast off 3 sts.

to make up
Join side and edging seams. Join elastic into a ring. Work a herringbone casing over rib at waist, enclosing elastic.

measurements
To fit ages 3–6 (6–9) months
finished measurements
Over nappy 51 (56) cm
Length 27 (30) cm

materials
2 (3) x 50g balls Debbie Bliss Baby Cashmerino in grey
Pair each 3 mm and 3.25 mm knitting needles
Waist length of 2 cm wide elastic

tension
25 sts and 34 rows to 10 cm square over st st using 3.25 mm needles

abbreviations
See page 25.

baby shorts

right leg

With 3 mm needles, cast on 66 (72) sts.
Rib row * K1, p1; rep from * to end.
Work a further 9 rows in rib.
Change to 3.25 mm needles.
Back shaping
Next 2 rows K6, turn, sl 1, p to end.
Next 2 rows K12, turn, sl 1, p to end.
Next 2 rows K18, turn, sl 1, p to end.
Next 2 rows K24, turn, sl 1, p to end.
Next 2 rows K30, turn, sl 1, p to end.
2nd size only
Next 2 rows K36, turn, sl 1, p to end.
Both sizes
Beg with a k row, cont in st st until work measures 17 (19) cm along short edge, ending with a p row.
**** Shape crotch**
Inc row (right side) K2, m1, k to last 2 sts, m1, k2.
P 1 row.
Rep the last 2 rows, 3 times more. **74 (80) sts.**
Cast on 3 sts at beg of next 2 rows. **80 (86) sts.**

Shape for legs

Work 2 rows in st st.

Dec row (right side) K2, skpo, k to last 4 sts, k2tog, k2.

Work 3 rows in st st.

Rep the last 4 rows, 4 (5) times more. **70 (74) sts.**

Leg edging

Change to 3mm needles.

Dec row K1 (3), [k2tog, k4] 11 times, k2tog, k1 (3). **58 (62) sts.**

P 1 row.

Eyelet row (right side) K1, [yf, k2tog] to last st, k1.

Work 2 rows in st st.

Cast off.

left leg

With 3mm needles, cast on 66 (72) sts.

Rib row * K1, p1; rep from * to end.

Work a further 9 rows in rib.

Change to 3.25mm needles.

Back shaping

Next 2 rows P6, turn, sl 1, k to end.

Next 2 rows P12, turn, sl 1, k to end.

Next 2 rows P18, turn, sl 1, k to end.

Next 2 rows P24, turn, sl 1, k to end.

Next 2 rows P30, turn, sl 1, k to end.

2nd size only

Next 2 rows P36, turn, sl 1, k to end.

Both sizes

Beg with a p row, cont in st st until work measures 17 (19) cm along short edge, ending with a p row.

Work as Right Leg from ** to end.

to make up

Join inner leg seams. Join centre front and back seam. Join elastic into a ring. Work a herringbone casing over rib at waist, enclosing elastic. Fold picot edge of legs onto wrong side and slip stitch in place.

cableblanket

measurements
Length 80cm
Width 50cm

materials
7 x 50g balls Debbie Bliss Cashmerino Double Knitting in pale blue
Long circular 3.25mm and 4mm knitting needles
Cable needle

tension
22 sts and 30 rows to 10cm square over st st using 4mm needles.

abbreviations
C8B = slip next 4 sts onto cable needle and leave at back of work, k4, then k4 from cable needle.
See page 25.

to make

With 3.25mm circular needle, cast on 142 sts.
K 8 rows.
Inc row K6, * p4, k4, m1, k2, m1, k4; rep from * to last 10 sts, p4, k6. **160 sts.**
Change to 4mm circular needle.
1st row (right side) K4, p2, k4, * p2, k8, p2, k4; rep from * to last 6 sts, p2, k4.
2nd row K6, * p4, k2, p4, k6; rep from * to last 10 sts, p4, k6.
3rd to 6th rows Rep 1st and 2nd rows twice more.
7th row K4, p2, k4, * p2, C8B, p2, k4; rep from * to last 6 sts, p2, k4.
8th row K6, * p4, k6, p4, k2; rep from * to last 10 sts, p4, k6.
9th row K4, p2, k4, * p2, k8, p2, k4; rep from * to last 6 sts, p2, k4.
10th to 18th rows Rep rows 8th and 9th rows four times more, then the 8th row again.
19th row K4, p2, k4, * p2, C8B, p2, k4; rep from * to last 6 sts, p2, k4.
20th row K6, * p4, k2, p4, k6; rep from * to last 10 sts, p4, k6.
21st row K4, p2, k4, * p2, k8, p2, k4; rep from * to last 6 sts, p2, k4.
22nd to 24th rows Rep 20th and 21st rows once more, then the 20th row again.
These 24 rows **form** the patt.
Cont in patt until blanket measures approximately 78cm from cast-on edge, ending with a 23rd row.
Dec row K6, * p4, k3, k2tog, k2, k2tog, k3; rep from * to last 10 sts, p4, k6. **142 sts.**
Change to 3.25mm circular needle.
K 8 rows.
Cast off.

teddy bear

size
Approximately 30cm tall

materials
2 x 50g balls Debbie Bliss Baby Cashmerino in stone
Pair 3mm knitting needles
Washable toy stuffing
Black felt and matching sewing thread

tension
27 sts and 56 rows to 10cm square over garter st
using 3mm needles

abbreviations
kfb = k into front and back of next st.
sk2togpo = slip 1, k2tog, pass slipped st over.
See page 25.

body

Make 2 pieces, beg at shoulders.
With 3mm needles, cast on 22 sts.
K 10 rows.
Cont in garter st and inc 1 st at each end of next row and 6 foll 6th rows. **36 sts.**
K 7 rows.
Shape base
Next row K1, skpo, k13, k2tog, skpo, k13, k2tog, k1. **32 sts.** K 1 row.
Next row K1, skpo, k11, k2tog, skpo, k11, k2tog, k1. **28 sts.** K 1 row.
Next row K1, skpo, k9, k2tog, skpo, k9, k2tog, k1. **24 sts.** K 1 row.
Cont to dec 4 sts on every alt row in this way until 8 sts rem. K 1 row.
Next row K1, sk2togpo, k3tog, k1. **4 sts.**
Next row [K2tog] twice.
Next row K2tog and fasten off.

head

Make 1 piece.
With 3mm needles, cast on 32 sts. K 2 rows.
Next row [Kfb, k6, kfb] 4 times. **40 sts.** K 1 row.
Next row [Kfb, k8, kfb] 4 times. **48 sts.** K 1 row.
Next row [Kfb, k10, kfb] 4 times. **56 sts.** K 30 rows.
Shape top
Next row [Skpo, k10, k2tog] 4 times. **48 sts.** K 1 row.
Next row [Skpo, k8, k2tog] 4 times. **40 sts.** K 1 row.
Next row [Skpo, k6, k2tog] 4 times. **32 sts.** K 1 row.
Next row [Skpo, k4, k2tog] 4 times. **24 sts.** K 1 row.
Next row [Skpo, k2, k2tog] 4 times. **16 sts.** K 1 row.
Next row [Skpo, k2tog] 4 times. **8 sts.** K 1 row.
Next row [Skpo, k2tog] twice. **4 sts.**
Break yarn, thread through rem sts, pull up and secure.

snout

Make 1 piece.
With 3mm needles, cast on 36 sts. K 10 rows.
Next row *K1, k2tog; rep from * to end. **24 sts.** K 1 row.
Next row [K2tog] to end. **12 sts.** K 1 row.
Break yarn, thread through sts, pull up and secure.

legs

Make 2 pieces.
With 3mm needles, cast on 8 sts. K 20 rows for the sole.
Shape foot
Cont in garter st and cast on 14 sts at beg of next 2 rows. **36 sts.** K 6 rows.
Dec 1 st at beg of next 10 rows. **26 sts.** K 30 rows.
Shape top
Next row K5, skpo, k2tog, k8, skpo, k2tog, k5. **22 sts.** K 1 row.
Next row K4, skpo, k2tog, k6, skpo, k2tog, k4. **18 sts.** K 1 row.
Next row K3, skpo, k2tog, k4, skpo, k2tog, k3. **14 sts.** K 1 row.

Next row K2, skpo, k2tog, k2, skpo, k2tog, k2. **10 sts.** K 1 row.
Next row K1, skpo, k2tog, skpo, k2tog, k1. **6 sts.**
Next row [K2tog] 3 times.
Next row K3tog and fasten off.

arms

Make 2 pieces.
With 3mm needles, cast on 4 sts. K 1 row.
Next row [Kfb] 3 times, k1. **7 sts.** K 1 row.
Next row [Kfb] 6 times, k1. **13 sts.** K 1 row.
Next row [Kfb] 12 times, k1. **25 sts.** K 36 rows.
Shape top
Next row K2tog tbl, k8, k2tog, k1, k2tog tbl, k8, k2tog. **21 sts.** K 1 row.
Next row K2tog tbl, k6, k2tog, k1, k2tog tbl, k6, k2tog. **17 sts.** K 1 row.
Next row K2tog tbl, k4, k2tog, k1, k2tog tbl, k4, k2tog. **13 sts.** K 1 row.
Next row K2tog tbl, k2, k2tog, k1, k2tog tbl, k2, k2tog. **9 sts.** K 1 row.
Next row K2tog tbl, k2tog, k1, k2tog tbl, k2tog. **5 sts.** K 1 row.
Next row K2tog tbl, k1, k2tog. **3 sts.**
Next row K3tog and fasten off.

ears

Make 2 pieces.
With 3mm needles, cast on 13 sts. K 4 rows.
Dec 1 st at each end of next row and 3 foll alt rows. **5 sts.** K 1 row.
Inc 1 st at each end of next row and 3 foll alt rows. **13 sts.** K 4 rows.
Cast off.

to make up

Join 2 body pieces together, leaving cast-on edges (shoulders) open. Evenly fill with stuffing, then join seam. Join back seam in head, leaving neck (cast-on edge) open. Evenly fill with stuffing. Join snout seam, leaving cast-on edge open. Position and sew onto head, stuffing lightly. Sew base of head onto shoulders. Fold each ear in half, position on head and sew in place. Join front seam of each leg, then sew sole in place, so leaving top of leg open. Evenly fill with stuffing, position on body and sew in place. Join arm seam, leaving top open, evenly fill with stuffing, position on body and sew in place. Cut two small circles from black felt for eyes and one quarter circle for the nose, then sew in place.

sizes
Approximately 8 (9: 10) cm for small (medium: large) hearts

materials
Oddments of 50g balls of Debbie Bliss Cotton DK in ecru (A), duck egg blue (B), lime (C) and pale pink (D)
Pair 4mm knitting needles
120cm narrow ribbon

tension
20 sts and 28 rows to 10cm square over st st using 4mm needles.

abbreviations
kfb = knit into front and back of next st.
See page 25.

heart mobile

note
The instructions are given for the basic heart shapes and the charts are given for the designs we used for our shapes. You can draw out the shapes on graph paper and create your own designs. Carry yarns not in use across wrong side of work and weave in yarns if carried over more than 4 sts. When working large spots, twist yarns at colour change to avoid holes forming.

basic hearts
(make 2 of each size)

With 4mm needles, cast on 2 sts.
1st row P2.
2nd row (right side) Kfb, kfb. 4 sts.
3rd row P.
4th row K1, m1, k to last st, m1, k1.
Rep the last 2 rows until there are 14 (16: 18) sts, ending with a right-side row.
Work 3 rows in st st.
Next row As 4th row. 16 (18: 20) sts.
Work 3 (5: 5) rows in st st.
Small and medium hearts only
Next row Ssk, k4 (5), k2tog, turn and cont on these 6 (7) sts only.
P 1 row.
Next row Ssk, k4 (5).
P 1 row.

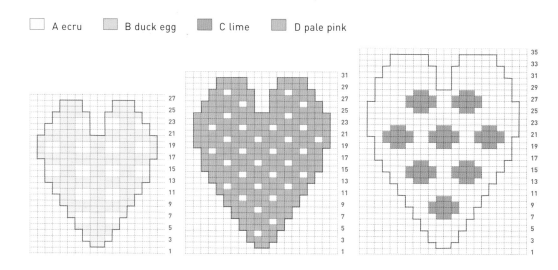

□ A ecru   ▨ B duck egg   ▨ C lime   ▨ D pale pink

Next row Ssk, k1 (2), k2tog.

P 1 row.

Cast off.

With right side facing, rejoin yarn to rem sts, ssk, k4 (5), k2tog.

P 1 row.

Next row K4 (5), k2tog.

P 1 row.

Next row Ssk, k1(2), k2tog.

P 1 row.

Cast off.

Large heart only

Next row Ssk, k to last 2 sts, k2tog. **18 sts.**

P 1 row.

Next row Ssk, k5, k2tog, turn and cont on these 7 sts only.

** Work 3 rows in st st.

Next row Ssk, k3, k2tog.

P 1 row.

Cast off. **

With right side facing, rejoin yarn to rem sts, ssk, k5, k2tog.

Work as first side from ** to **.

to make up

Join hearts together in pairs around their outer edges. Thread the ribbon through the small heart from top to bottom, leaving a loop at the top. Tie the two ends together under the heart to prevent it slipping down the ribbon. Thread the ribbon ends through the medium heart and tie at the base, then thread through the large heart and tie.

size
Approximately 90 x 110cm

materials
15 x 50g balls Debbie Bliss Baby Cashmerino in ecru (M)
Oddments of contrast yarn (C) for embroidery
3mm and 3.25mm circular knitting needles
Cable needle

tension
25 sts and 34 rows to 10cm square over st st using 3.25mm needles.

sampler blanket

abbreviations

C4B = slip next 2 sts onto cable needle and hold at back of work, k2, then k2 from cable needle.
C4F = slip next 2 sts onto cable needle and hold at front of work, k2, then k2 from cable needle.
C5F = slip next 3 sts onto cable needle and hold at front of work, k2, then slip the p st from cable needle back onto left-hand needle, p this st, then k2 from cable needle.
C6B = slip next 3 sts onto cable needle and hold at back of work, k3, then k3 from cable needle.
C6F = slip next 3 sts onto cable needle and hold at front of work, k3, then k3 from cable needle.
C3BP = slip next st onto cable needle and hold at back of work, k2, then p1 from cable needle.
C3FP = slip next 2 sts onto cable needle and hold at front of work, p1, then k2 from cable needle.
C4BP = slip next 2 sts onto cable needle and hold at back of work, k2, then p2 from cable needle.
C4FP = slip next 2 sts onto cable needle and hold at front of work, p2, then k2 from cable needle.
C5BP = slip next 2 sts onto cable needle and hold at back of work, k3, then p2 from cable needle.
C5FP = slip next 3 sts onto cable needle and hold at front of work, p2, then k3 from cable needle.
T5L = slip next 2 sts onto cable needle and hold at front of work, k2, p1, then k2 from cable needle.
MB = k into front, back and front of next st, [turn and k3] 3 times, turn and sl 1, k2tog, psso.
Also see page 25.

motif A
(worked over 40 sts)

1st row (right side) P9, T5L, p12, T5L, p9.
2nd row K9, p2, k1, p2, k12, p2, k1, p2, k9.
3rd row P8, C3BP, k1, C3FP, p10, C3BP, k1, C3FP, p8.
4th row K8, p2, k1, p1, k1, p2, k10, p2, k1, p1, k1, p2, k8.
5th row P7, C3BP, k1, p1, k1, C3FP, p8, C3BP, k1, p1, k1, C3FP, p7.
6th row K7, p2, [k1, p1] twice, k1, p2, k8, p2, [k1, p1] twice, k1, p2, k7.
7th row P6, C3BP, [k1, p1] twice, k1, C3FP, p6, C3BP, [k1, p1] twice, k1, C3FP, p6.
8th row K6, p2, [k1, p1] 3 times, k1, p2, k6, p2, [k1, p1] 3 times, k1, p2, k6.
9th row P5, C3BP, [k1, p1] 3 times, k1, C3FP, p4, C3BP, [k1, p1] 3 times, k1, C3FP, p5.
10th row K5, p2, [k1, p1] 4 times, k1, p2, k4, p2, [k1, p1] 4 times, k1, p2, k5.
11th row P4, C3BP, [k1, p1] 4 times, k1, C3FP, p2, C3BP, [k1, p1] 4 times, k1, C3FP, p4.
12th row K4, p2, [k1, p1] 5 times, k1, p2, k2, p2, [k1, p1] 5 times, k1, p2, k4.
13th to 36th rows Rep 1st to 12th rows twice more.
37th row P4, k3, [p1, k1] 4 times, p1, k3, p2, k3, [p1, k1] 4 times, p1, k3, p4.
38th row K4, p3, [k1, p1] 4 times, k1, p3, k2, p3, [k1, p1] 4 times, k1, p3, k4.

motif B
(worked over 40 sts)

1st row (right side) P9, C3BP, p5, C6B, p5, C3FP, p9.
2nd row K9, p2, k6, p6, k6, p2, k9.
3rd row P8, C3BP, p4, C5BP, C5FP, p4, C3FP, p8.
4th row K8, p2, k5, p3, k4, p3, k5, p2, k8.
5th row P7, C3BP, p3, C5BP, p4, C5FP, p3, C3FP, p7.
6th row K7, p2, k1, MB, k2, p3, k8, p3, k2, MB, k1, p2, k7.
7th row P7, C3FP, p3, k3, p8, k3, p3, C3BP, p7.
8th row K8, p2, k3, p3, k8, p3, k3, p2, k8.

9th row P8, C3FP, p2, C5FP, p4, C5BP, p2, C3BP, p8.
10th row K9, p2, [k4, p3] twice, k4, p2, k9.
11th row P9, C3FP, p3, C5FP, C5BP, p3, C3BP, p9.
12th row K8, MB, k1, p2, k5, p6, k5, p2, k1, MB, k8.
13th to 38th rows Rep 1st to 12th twice more, then 1st and 2nd rows again.

motif C
(worked over 40 sts)

1st row (right side) P10, C5F, p10, C5F, p10.
2nd row K10, p2, k1, p2, k10, p2, k1, p2, k10.
3rd row P9, C3BP, k1, C3FP, p8, C3BP, k1, C3FP, p9.
4th row K9, p2, k1, p1, k1, p2, k8, p2, k1, p1, k1, p2, k9.
5th row P8, C3BP, k1, p1, k1, C3FP, p6, C3BP, k1, p1, k1, C3FP, p8.
6th row K8, p2, [k1, p1] twice, k1, p2, k6, p2, [k1, p1] twice, k1, p2, k8.
7th row P7, C3BP, [k1, p1] twice, k1, C3FP, p4, C3BP, [k1, p1] twice, k1, C3FP, p7.
8th row K7, p2, [k1, p1] 3 times, k1, p2, k4, p2, [k1, p1] 3 times, k1, p2, k7.
9th row P6, C3BP, [k1, p1] 3 times, k1, C3FP, p2, C3BP, [k1, p1] 3 times, k1, C3FP, p6.
10th row K6, p2, [k1, p1] 4 times, k1, p2, k2, p2, [k1, p1] 4 times, k1, p2, k6.
11th row P6, C3FP, [p1, k1] 3 times, p1, C3BP, p2, C3FP, [p1, k1] 3 times, p1, C3BP, p6.
12th row As 8th row.
13th row P7, C3FP, [p1, k1] twice, p1, C3BP, p4, C3FP, [p1, k1] twice, p1, C3BP, p7.
14th row As 6th row.
15th row P8, C3FP, p1, k1, p1, C3BP, p6, C3FP, p1, k1, p1, C3BP, p8.
16th row As 4th row.
17th row P9, C3FP, p1, C3BP, p8, C3FP, p1, C3BP, p9.
18th row As 2nd row.
19th to 38th rows Rep 1st to 18th rows once more then 1st and 2nd rows again.

motif D
(worked over 40 sts)

1st row P8, k2, p8, C4B, p8, k2, p8.
2nd row K8, p2, k8, p4, k8, p2, k8.
3rd row P8, C4FP, p4, C4BP, C4FP, p4, C4BP, p8.
4th row K10, [p2, k4] 3 times, p2, k10.
5th row P10, C4FP, C4BP, p4, C4FP, C4BP, p10.
6th row K12, p4, k8, p4, k12.
7th row P12, C4B, p4, MB, p3, C4F, p12.
8th row As 6th row.
9th row P10, C4BP, C4FP, p4, C4BP, C4FP, p10.
10th row As 4th row.
11th row P8, C4BP, p4, C4FP, C4BP, p4, C4FP, p8.
12th row As 2nd row.
13th row P8, k2, p4, MB, p3, C4B, p4, MB, p3, k2, p8.
14th row K8, p2, k8, p4, k8, p2, k8.
15th to 26th rows Rep 3rd to 14th rows once more.
27th to 36th rows Rep 3rd to 12th rows.
37th and 38th rows As 1st and 2nd rows.

to make

With 3mm circular needle and M, cast on 240 sts.
K 19 rows.
1st row K10, [p1, k1] to last 12 sts, p1, k11.
2nd row K11, [p1, k1] to last 11 sts, p1, k10.
Rep the last 2 rows 3 times more.
Change to 3.25mm circular needle.

First row of motifs

1st row (right side) K10, moss st 5, [p38, moss st 5] to last 53 sts, k38, moss st 5, k10.
2nd row K10, moss st 5, p38, moss st 5, [k38, moss st 5] to last 10 sts, k10.
3rd row As 1st row.
4th (inc) row (wrong side) K10, moss st 5, p38, moss st 5, k18, m1, k2, m1, k18, moss st 5, k11, m1, k16, m1, k11, moss st, 5, k18, m1, k2, m1, k18, moss st 5, k10, m1, k18, m1, k10, moss st 5, k10. **248 sts.**
5th row K10, moss st 5, work across 1st row of motif A, moss st 5, work across 1st row of motif D, moss st 5, work across 1st row of motif C, moss st 5, work across 1st row of motif B, moss st 5, k38, moss st 5, k10.
6th row K10, moss st 5, p38, moss st 5, work across 2nd row of motif B, moss st 5, work across 2nd row of motif C, moss st 5, work across 2nd row of motif D, moss st 5, work across 2nd row of motif A, moss st 5, k10.
The last 2 rows set the position of the motifs with moss st between and garter st edging.
Working correct patt rows, work a further 36 rows.
43rd (dec) row K10, moss st 5, p9, p2tog, p18, p2tog, p9, moss st 5, p18, [p2tog] twice, p18, moss st 5, p10, p2tog, p16, p2tog, p10, moss st 5, p18, [p2tog] twice, p18, moss st 5, k38, moss st 5, k10. **240 sts.**
44th row K10, moss st 5, p38, moss st 5, [k38, moss st 5] to last 10 sts, k10.
45th and 46th rows As 1st and 2nd rows.
Change to 3mm circular needle.
1st row K10, [p1, k1] to last 12 sts, p1, k11.
2nd row K11, [p1, k1] to last 11 sts, p1, k10.
Rep the last 2 rows 3 times more.
Change to 3.25mm circular needle.

** Second row of motifs

1st row (right side) K10, moss st 5, [p38, moss st 5] to last 10 sts, k10.
2nd row K10, moss st 5, [k38, moss st 5] to last 10 sts, k10.
3rd row As 1st row.
4th (inc) row (wrong side) K10, moss st 5, k18, m1, k2, m1, k18, moss st 5, k11, m1, k16, m1, k11, moss st 5, k18, m1, k2, m1, k18, moss st 5, k10, m1, k18, m1, k10, moss st 5, k18, m1, k2, m1, k18, moss st 5, k10. **250 sts.**
5th row K10, moss st 5, work across 1st row of motif B, moss st 5, work across 1st row of motif A, moss st 5, work across 1st row of motif D, moss st 5, work across 1st row of motif C, moss st 5, work across 1st row of motif B, moss st 5, k10.
6th row K10, moss st 5, work across 2nd row of motif B, moss st 5, work across 2nd row of motif C, moss st 5, work across 2nd row of motif D, moss st 5, work across 2nd row of motif A, moss st 5, work across 2nd row of motif B, moss st 5, k10.
The last 2 rows set the position of the motifs with moss st between and garter st edging.

● ● ● ● ● ● ● ● ● ● ● ▷

Working correct patt rows, work a further 36 rows.

43rd (dec) row K10, moss st 5, p18, [p2tog] twice, p18, moss st 5, p9, p2tog, p18, p2tog, p9, moss st 5, p18, [p2tog] twice, p18, moss st 5, p10, p2tog, p16, p2tog, p10, moss st 5, p18, [p2tog] twice, p18, moss st 5, k10. **240 sts.**

44th row K10, moss st 5, [k38, moss st 5] to last 10 sts, k10.

45th and 46th rows As 1st and 2nd rows.

Change to 3mm circular needle.

1st row K10, [p1, k1] to last 12 sts, p1, k11.

2nd row K11, [p1, k1] to last 11 sts, p1, k10.

Rep the last 2 rows 3 times more.

Change to 3.25mm circular needle.

Third row of motifs

1st row (right side) K10, moss st 5, [p38, moss st 5] to last 10 sts, k10.

2nd row K10, moss st 5, [k38, moss st 5] to last 10 sts, k10.

3rd row As 1st row.

4th (inc) row (wrong side) K10, moss st 5, k11, m1, k16, m1, k11, moss st, 5, k18, m1, k2, m1, k18, moss st 5, k10, m1, k18, m1, k10, moss st 5, k18, m1, k2, m1, k18, moss st 5, k11, m1, k16, m1, k11, moss st 5, k10. **250 sts.**

5th row K10, moss st 5, work across 1st row of motif C, moss st 5, work across 1st row of motif B, moss st 5, work across 1st row of motif A, moss st 5, work across 1st row of motif D, moss st 5, work across 1st row of motif C, moss st 5, k10.

6th row K10, moss st 5, work across 2nd row of motif C, moss st 5, work across 2nd row of motif D, moss st 5, work across 2nd row of motif A, moss st 5, work across 2nd row of motif B, moss st 5, work across 2nd row of motif C, moss st 5, k10.

The last 2 rows **set** the position of the motifs with moss st between and garter st edging.

Working correct patt rows, work a further 36 rows.

43rd (dec) row K10, moss st 5, p10, p2tog, p16, p2tog, p10, moss st 5, p18, [p2tog] twice, p18, moss st 5, p9, p2tog, p18, p2tog, p9, moss st 5, p18, [p2tog] twice, p18, moss st 5, p10, p2tog, p16, p2tog, p10, moss st 5, k10. **240 sts.**

44th row K10, moss st 5, [k38, moss st 5] to last 10 sts, k10.

45th and 46th rows As 1st and 2nd rows.

Change to 3mm circular needle.

1st row K10, [p1, k1] to last 12 sts, p1, k11.

2nd row K11, [p1, k1] to last 11 sts, p1, k10.

Rep the last 2 rows 3 times more. **

Change to 3.25mm circular needle.

Fourth row of motifs

1st row (right side) K10, moss st 5, [p38, moss st 5] to last 10 sts, k10.

2nd row K10, moss st 5, [k38, moss st 5] to last 10 sts, k10.

3rd row As 1st row.

4th (inc) row (wrong side) K10, moss st, 5, k18, m1, k2, m1, k18, moss st 5, k10, m1, k18, m1, k10, moss st 5, k18, m1, k2, m1, k18, moss st 5, k11, m1, k16, m1, k11, moss st 5, k18, m1, k2, m1, k18, moss st 5, k10. **250 sts**

5th row K10, work across 1st row of motif D, moss st 5, work across 1st row of motif C, moss st 5,

work across 1st row of motif B, moss st 5, work across 1st row of motif A, moss st 5, work across 1st row of motif D, moss st 5, k10.

6th row K10, moss st 5, work across 2nd row of motif D, moss st 5, work across 2nd row of motif A, moss st 5, work across 2nd row of motif B, moss st 5, work across 2nd row of motif C, moss st 5, work across 2nd row of motif D, moss st 5, k10.

The last 2 rows **set** the position of the motifs with moss st between and garter st edging.

Working correct patt rows, work a further 36 rows.

43rd (dec) row K10, moss st 5, p18, [p2tog] twice, p18, moss st 5, p10, p2tog, p16, p2tog, p10, moss st 5, p18, [p2tog] twice, p18, moss st 5, p9, p2tog, p18, p2tog, p9, moss st 5, p18, [p2tog] twice, p18, moss st 5, k10. **240 sts.**

44th row K10, moss st 5, [k38, moss st 5] to last 10 sts, k10.

45th and 46th rows As 1st and 2nd rows.

● ● ● ● ● ● ● ● ● ● ● ▶

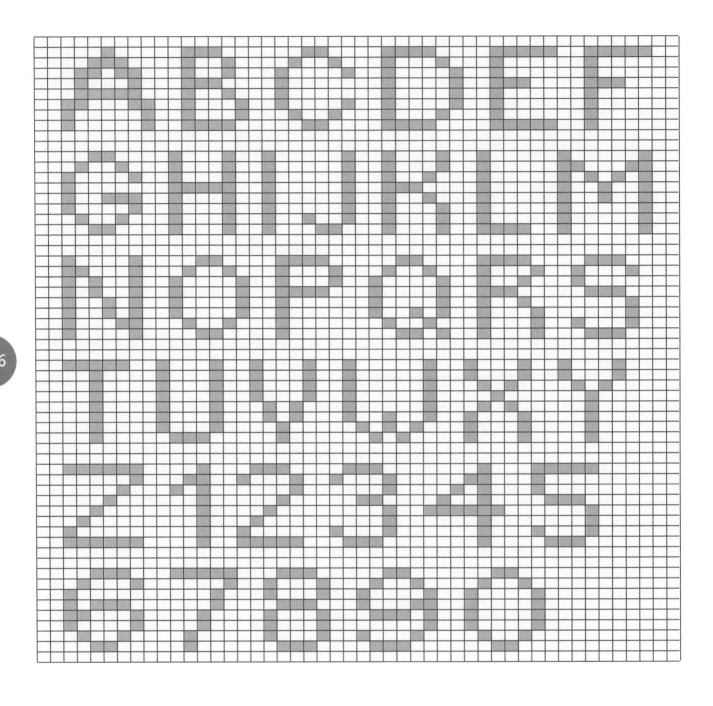

Change to 3mm circular needle.

1st row K10, [p1, k1] to last 12 sts, p1, k11.

2nd row K11, [p1, k1] to last 11 sts, p1, k10.

Rep the last 2 rows 3 times more.

Change to 3.25mm circular needle.

Fifth row of motifs

1st row (right side) K10, moss st 5, [p38, moss st 5] to last 10 sts, k10.

2nd row K10, moss st 5, [k38, moss st 5] to last 10 sts, k10.

3rd row As 1st row.

4th (inc) row (wrong side) K10, moss st 5, k10, m1, k18, m1, k10, moss st 5, k18, m1, k2, m1, k18, moss st 5, k11, m1, k16, m1, k11, moss st 5, k18, m1, k2, m1, k18, moss st 5, k10, m1, k18, m1, k10, moss st 5, k10. **250 sts.**

5th row K10, moss st 5, work across 1st row of motif A, moss st 5, work across 1st row of motif D, moss st 5, work across 1st row of motif C, moss st 5, work across 1st row of motif B, moss st 5, work across 1st row of motif A, moss st 5, k10.

6th row K10, moss st 5, work across 2nd row of motif A, moss st 5, work across 2nd row of motif B, moss st 5, work across 2nd row of motif C, moss st 5, work across 2nd row of motif D, moss st 5, work across 2nd row of motif A, moss st 5, k10.

The last 2 rows **set** the position of the motifs with moss st between and garter st edging.

Working correct patt rows, work a further 36 rows.

43rd (dec) row K10, moss st 5, p9, p2tog, p18, p2tog, p9, moss st 5, p18, [p2tog] twice, p18, moss st 5, p10, p2tog, p16, p2tog, p10, moss st 5, p18, [p2tog] twice, p18, moss st 5, p9, p2tog, p18, p2tog, p9, moss st 5, k10. **240 sts.**

44th row K10, moss st 5, [k38, moss st 5] to last 10 sts, k10.

45th and 46th rows As 1st and 2nd rows.

Change to 3mm circular needle.

1st row K10, [p1, k1] to last 12 sts, p1, k11.

2nd row K11, [p1, k1] to last 11 sts, p1, k10.

Rep the last 2 rows 3 times more.

Change to 3.25mm circular needle.

Sixth and seventh rows of motifs

Work as Second and Third row of motifs from ** to **.

K 19 rows.

Cast off.

embroidery

Using your own selection of letters and numbers from the Chart opposite and contrast yarn (C), Swiss darn the initials and date onto the blank square at the lower left-hand corner.

fairisle
hangers

size
To fit a 22cm plain wooden coathanger

materials
1 x 50g ball (or oddments) Debbie Bliss Baby Cashmerino in each of pale pink, lime, teal, duck egg, ecru, red and pink
Pair 3.25mm knitting needles
22cm plain wooden coathangers
Polyester wadding
30cm of narrow ribbon

tension
25 sts and 34 rows to 10cm over fairisle st st using 3.25mm needles.

abbreviations
See page 25.

note
You may find it difficult to obtain 22cm coathangers, but you can easily cut down a standard width hanger to size using a hacksaw. If you want to cover a hanger of a different width, you will need to recalculate the number of sts. The pattern is worked over a multiple of 8 sts, plus 1 edge st.

to make

With 3.25mm needles and main colour from your chosen chart, cast on 57 sts.
Beg with a k row, work 2 rows in st st.
Now cont in st st and work from chart as follows:
1st chart row (right side) K1 edge st, [k8 patt rep sts] 7 times.
2nd chart row [P8 patt rep sts] 7 times, p1 edge st.
These 2 rows **set** the position of the chart and are repeated.
Cont until all 15 chart rows have been worked, then rep these 15 rows once more.
Cast off.

to finish

Pad a coathanger with wadding and stitch in place. Fold knitting in half matching cast-on and cast-off edges and join side seams from fold to edge. Find the centre of the cover and thread hanger hook through at this point. Ease cover over hanger and join cast-on to cast-off edges. Tie a ribbon around base of hook.

	pale pink		lime		teal		duck egg		ecru		red		pink

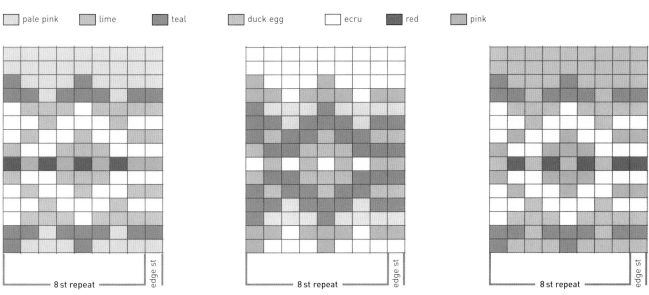

8 st repeat — edge st

8 st repeat — edge st

8 st repeat — edge st

232 cabletanktop

measurements
To fit ages 3–6 (6–9: 9–12: 12–18: 18–24) months
actual measurements
Chest 45 (48: 52: 56: 60)cm
Length to shoulder 22 (24: 26: 30: 32)cm

materials
2 (2: 2: 3: 3) x 50g balls Debbie Bliss Baby Cashmerino in indigo
Pair each 3mm and 3.25mm knitting needles
3mm circular needle
Cable needle
2 small buttons

tension
32 sts and 34 rows to 10cm square over patt using 3.25mm needles.

abbreviations
C4B = slip next 2 sts onto cable needle and hold at back of work, k2,
then k2 from cable needle.
See page 25.

back

** With 3.25mm needles, cast on 74 (80: 86: 92: 98) sts.

1st row (right side) [K2, p1] 1 (2: 3: 4: 5) times, [k4, p1, k2, p1] 8 times, k4, [p1, k2] 1 (2: 3: 4: 5) times.

2nd row [P2, k1] 1 (2: 3: 4: 5) times, [p4, k1, p2, k1] 8 times, p4, [k1, p2] 1 (2: 3: 4: 5) times.

3rd row [K2, p1] 1 (2: 3: 4: 5) times, [C4B, p1, k2, p1] 8 times, C4B, [p1, k2] 1 (2: 3: 4: 5) times.

4th row As 2nd row.

These 4 rows form the cable and rib patt and are repeated throughout.

Work in patt until back measures 12 (13: 14: 17: 19)cm from cast-on edge, ending with a wrong side row.

Shape armholes

Cast off 4 (4: 5: 5: 6) sts at beg of next 2 rows. 66 (72: 76: 82: 86) sts.

Dec 1 st at each end of the next and 5 (5: 7: 7: 7) foll alt rows. 54 (60: 60: 66: 70) sts.**

Cont straight in patt as now set until back measures 17 (19: 21: 24: 26)cm from cast-on edge, ending with a wrong side row.

Divide for neck opening

Next row Patt 24 (27: 27: 30: 32), turn and cast on 5 sts.

Cont on these 29 (32: 32: 35: 37) sts only for first side of neck, leave rem sts on a spare needle.

Next row (wrong side) K1, p3, k1, patt to end.

Next row Patt to last 5 sts, p1, k3, p1.

Rep these 2 rows until back measures 21 (23: 25: 29: 31)cm from cast-on edge, ending with a wrong side row.

Shape back neck

Next 2 rows Patt to last 10 sts, slip these sts onto a holder, turn and patt to end.

Next 2 rows Patt to last 5 sts, slip these sts onto same holder, turn and patt to end.

14 (17: 17: 20: 22) sts.

Cast off rem sts for shoulder, working 2 sts tog in centre of each cable.

With right side facing, rejoin yarn to 30 (33: 33: 36: 38) sts on spare needle, patt to end.

Patt 7 rows.

Buttonhole row (right side) P1, k1, yf, k2tog, patt to end.

Cont in patt until back measures 21 (23: 25: 29: 31)cm from cast-on edge, ending with a wrong side row.

Shape back neck

Next row (right side) Patt 11 and slip these sts onto a holder, patt to end.

Patt 1 row.

Next row Patt 5 and slip these sts onto the same holder, patt to end.

Patt 1 row. 14 (17: 17: 20: 22) sts.

Cast off rem sts for shoulder, working 2 sts tog in centre of each cable.

front

Work as given for Back from ** to **.

Cont straight in patt until front measures 16 (18: 20: 23: 25)cm from cast-on edge, ending with a wrong side row.

Shape neck

Next row Patt 21 (24: 24: 27: 29) sts, turn and work on these sts only for first side of front neck.

Next row (wrong side) Cast off 2 sts, patt to end.

Patt 1 row.

Rep the last 2 rows once more.

Next row (wrong side) P1, p2tog, patt to end.

Next row Patt to last 2 sts, k2.

Rep the last 2 rows twice more. **14 (17: 17: 20: 22) sts.**

Cont straight until front measures same as Back to shoulder, ending with a wrong side row.

Cast off, working 2 sts tog in centre of each cable.

With right side facing, slip centre 12 sts onto a holder, rejoin yarn to rem sts, patt to end.

Patt 1 row.

Next row Cast off 2 sts, patt to end.

Patt 1 row.

Rep the last 2 rows once more.

Next row K1, skpo, patt to end.

Next row Patt to last 2 sts, p2.

Rep the last 2 rows twice more. **14 (17: 17: 20: 22) sts.**

Work straight until front measures same as Back to shoulder, ending with a right side row.

neckband

Cast off, working 2 sts tog in centre of each cable.

Join shoulder seams.

With right side facing and 3mm circular needle, work across 16 sts on left back neck holder as follows: [p1, patt 4, p1, k2] twice, then pick up 2 sts at back neck edge to shoulder, and k16 (19: 19: 22: 22) sts down left front neck, work [p1, k2, p1, k4, p1, k2, p1] across 12 sts from front neck holder, now pick up and k16 (19: 19: 22: 22) sts up right front neck, 2 sts from back neck edge then work across 15 sts on right back neck holder as follows: k2, p1, patt 4, p1, k2, p1, k3, p1. **79 (85: 85: 91: 91) sts.**

1st row (wrong side) K1, p3, k1, p2, k1, p4, [k1, p2] 8 (9: 9: 10: 10) times, k1, p4, k1, [p2, k1] 8 (9: 9: 10: 10) times, p4, k1, p2, k1, p4, k1.

Buttonhole row P1, k1, yf, k2tog, k1, p1, k2, p1, C4B, [p1, k2] 8 (9: 9: 10: 10) times, p1, C4B, p1, [k2, p1] 8 (9: 9: 10: 11) times, C4B, p1, k2, p1, k3, p1.

3rd row As 1st row.

4th row [P1, k4, p1, k2] twice, [p1, k2] 7 (8: 8: 9: 9) times, p1, k4, p1, [k2, p1] 8 (9: 9: 10: 10) times, k4, p1, k2, p1, k3, p1.

Cast off in patt, working [p2tog] twice across each cable while casting off.

armbands

With right side facing and 3mm needles, pick up and k62 (68: 74: 86: 92) sts evenly around armhole edge.

1st row (wrong side) [P2, k1] 3 (4: 5: 7: 8) times, [p4, k1, p2, k1] 5 times, p4, [k1, p2] 3 (4: 5: 7: 8) times.

2nd row [K2, p1] 3 (4: 5: 7: 8) times, [k4, p1, k2, p1] 5 times, k4, [p1, k2] 3 (4: 5: 7: 8) times.

3rd row As 1st row.

4th row [K2, p1] 3 (4: 5: 7: 8) times, [C4B, p1, k2, p1] 5 times, C4B, [p1, k2] 3 (4: 5: 7: 8) times.

Cast off in patt, working [p2tog] twice across each cable while casting off.

to make up

Join side and armband seams. Stitch cast-on sts at back opening behind buttonhole band. Sew on buttons.

striped cardigan

measurements
To fit ages 3–6 (6–9: 9–12: 12–18: 18–24) months
actual measurements
Chest 51 (56: 60: 65: 70)cm
Length to shoulder 24 (26: 28: 32: 36)cm
Sleeve length 15 (17: 19: 22: 24)cm

materials
2 (2: 2: 3: 3) x 50g balls Debbie Bliss Baby Cashmerino in each of grey (M) and ecru (C)
Pair each 3mm and 3.25mm knitting needles
3mm circular knitting needle
6 (6: 6: 7: 7) buttons

tension
25 sts and 34 rows to 10cm square over st st using 3.25mm needles.

abbreviations
See page 25.

back

With 3mm needles and C, cast on 65 (71: 77: 83: 89) sts.
1st rib row K1, [p1, k1] to end.
Change to M.
2nd rib row P1, [k1, p1] to end.
With M, rep the last 2 rows twice more.
Change to 3.25mm needles.
Beg with a k row, work in st st and stripes of 2 rows C and 2 rows M, until back measures
14 (15: 16: 19: 22)cm from cast-on edge, ending with a p row.
Shape armholes
Keeping st st stripes correct as set throughout, cast off 3 (3: 3: 4: 4) sts at beg of next 2 rows.
Next row K2, skpo, k to last 4 sts, k2tog, k2.
Next row P to end.
Rep the last 2 rows 3 (4: 5: 5: 6) times. **51 (55: 59: 63: 67) sts.**
Cont straight until back measures 24 (26: 28: 32: 36)cm from cast-on edge, ending with a p row.
Shape shoulders
Cast off 12 (13: 14: 15: 16) sts at beg of next 2 rows.
Leave rem 27 (29: 31: 33: 35) sts on a holder.

left front

With 3mm needles and C, cast on 33 (35: 39: 41: 45) sts.
1st rib row P1, [k1, p1] to end.
Change to M.
2nd rib row K1, [p1, k1] to end.
With M, rep the last 2 rows twice more.
Change to 3.25mm needles. **
Beg with a k row, work in st st and stripes of 2 rows C and 2 rows M until front measures
14 (15: 16: 19: 22)cm from cast-on edge, ending with the same stripe row as Back.
Shape armhole
Keeping st st stripes correct as set throughout, cast off 3 (3: 3: 4: 4) sts at beg of next row.
Work 1 row.
Next row K2, skpo, k to end.
Next row P to end.
Rep the last 2 rows 3 (4: 5: 5: 6) times. **26 (27: 30: 31: 34) sts.**
Cont straight until front measures 19 (21: 22: 26: 29)cm from cast-on edge, ending with a p row.
Shape neck
Next row K to last 4 (5: 5: 5: 6) sts and leave these sts on a holder.
Dec 1 st at neck edge on every row until 12 (13: 14: 15: 16) sts rem.
Cont straight until front measures same as Back to shoulder, ending at armhole edge.
Shape shoulder
Cast off.

right front

Work as given for Left Front to **.
Beg with a k row, cont in st st and stripes of 2 rows C and 2 rows M until front measures
14 (15: 16: 19: 22)cm from cast-on edge, working one more row than on Left Front.
Shape armhole
Keeping st st stripes correct as set throughout, cast off 3 (3: 3: 4: 4) sts at beg of next row.
Next row K to last 4 sts, k2tog, k2.
Next row P to end.
Rep the last 2 rows 3 (4: 5: 5: 6) times. **26 (27: 30: 31: 34) sts.**
Cont straight until front measures 19 (21: 22: 26: 29)cm from cast-on edge, ending with a p row.
Shape neck
Next row K4 (5: 5: 5: 6) sts, leave these sts on a holder, k to end.
Dec 1 st at neck edge on every row until 12 (13: 14: 15: 16) sts rem.
Cont straight until front measures same as Back to shoulder, ending at armhole edge.
Shape shoulder
Cast off.

sleeves

With 3mm needles and C, cast on 34 (36: 38: 40: 42) sts.
1st rib row [K1, p1] to end.
Change to M.
With M, rep the last row 5 times more.
Change to 3.25mm needles.
Beg with a k row, work in st st and stripes of 2 rows C and 2 rows M and **at the same time** inc
1 st at each end of the 3rd row and every foll 4th row until there are 54 (56: 60: 68: 74) sts.
Working in st st stripes as set throughout, cont straight until sleeve measures 15 (17: 19: 22:
24)cm from cast-on edge, ending with the same stripe row as on Back to armhole.
Shape sleeve top
Cast off 3 (3: 3: 4: 4) sts at beg of next 2 rows.
Next row K2, skpo, k to last 4 sts, k2tog, k2.
Next row P to end.
Rep the last 2 rows 3 (4: 5: 5: 6) times. **40 (40: 42: 48: 52) sts.**
Cast off.

neckband

Join shoulder seams.
With right side facing, 3mm needles and M, slip 4 (5: 5: 5: 6) sts on right front holder onto a
needle, pick up and k17 (17: 18: 19: 19) sts up right front neck, k27 (29: 31: 33: 35) sts from back
neck holder, pick up and k17 (17: 18: 19: 19) sts down left front neck, then k4 (5: 5: 5: 6) sts from
left front holder. **69 (73: 77: 81: 85) sts.**
1st row P1, [k1, p1] to end.
2nd row K1, [p1, k1] to end.
These 2 rows **form** the rib.
Work 3 rows more in rib.
Change to C.
Rib 1 row.
Cast off in rib.

button band	With right side facing, 3mm needles and M, pick up and k55 (61: 63: 71: 77) sts along left front edge.

Work 5 rows in rib as given for Neckband.
Change to C.
Rib 1 row.
Cast off in rib.

buttonhole band

With right side facing, 3mm needles and M, pick up and k55 (61: 63: 71: 77) sts along right front edge.
Work 2 rows in rib as given for Neckband.
Buttonhole row Rib 1 (2: 3: 1: 1), [rib 2tog, yf, rib 8 (9: 9: 9: 10) sts] 5 (5: 5: 6: 6) times, rib 2tog, yf, rib 2 (2: 3: 2: 2).
Rib 2 rows.
Change to C.
Rib 1 row.
Cast off in rib.

to make up

Sew sleeves into armholes, matching stripes on shaping and easing cast-off edge to fit.
Join side and sleeve seams. Sew on buttons.

size
To fit ages 3–6 months

materials
1 x 50g ball Debbie Bliss Baby Cashmerino in each of grey (M) and ecru (C)
Pair 2.75mm knitting needles

tension
28 sts and 37 rows to 10cm square over st st using 2.75mm needles.

abbreviations
See page 25.

striped bootees

to make

With 2.75mm needles and M, cast on 36 sts and k 1 row.
1st row (right side) K1, yf, k16, yf, [k1, yf] twice, k16, yf, k1.
2nd and all wrong side rows K to end, working k1 tbl into each yf of previous row.
3rd row K2, yf, k16, yf, k2, yf, k3, yf, k16, yf, k2.
5th row K3, yf, k16, yf, [k4, yf] twice, k16, yf, k3.
7th row K4, yf, k16, yf, k5, yf, k6, yf, k16, yf, k4.
9th row K5, yf, k16, yf, [k7, yf] twice, k16, yf, k5.
11th row K22, yf, k8, yf, k9, yf, k22. 64 sts.
12th row As 2nd row.
Beg with a k row, cont in st st stripes of 2 rows C, 2 rows M throughout as follows:
Work 10 rows.
Shape instep
Next row K36, skpo, turn.
Next row Sl 1, p8, p2tog, turn.
Next row Sl 1, k8, skpo, turn.
Rep the last 2 rows 7 times more, then work first of the 2 rows again.
Next row Sl 1, k to end.
Next row P17, p2tog, p8, p2tog tbl, p17. 44 sts.
Break off C and cont in M only.
Next row [K1, p1] to end.
Rep the last row 11 times more.
Change to C.
Rib 1 row and cast off in rib.

to finish

Join sole and back seam.

crossover jacket

measurements
To fit ages 3–6 (6–9: 9–12: 12–18: 18–24) months
actual measurements
Chest 50 (53: 60: 63: 70)cm
Length to shoulder 24 (26: 29: 32: 36)cm
Sleeve length 14 (16: 18: 20: 22)cm

materials
3 (4: 4: 5: 5) x 50g balls Debbie Bliss Cashmerino Aran in stone (M) and 1 x 50g ball in teal (C)
Pair each 4.50mm and 5mm knitting needles
One button
50cm ribbon or leather thonging

tension
24 sts and 24 rows to 10cm square over rib using 5mm needles

abbreviations
See page 25.

back

With 5mm needles and C, cast on 62 (66: 74: 78: 86) sts.
1st row (right side) K2, * p2, k2; rep from * to end.
2nd row P2, * k2, p2; rep from * to end.
These 2 rows **form** the rib.
Change to M.
Cont in rib until back measures 14 (15: 17: 19: 22)cm from cast-on edge, ending with a wrong side row.
Shape armholes
Cast on 1 st at beg of next 2 rows. **64 (68: 76: 80: 88) sts.**
Cont in rib until back measures 24 (26: 29: 32: 36)cm from cast-on edge, ending with a wrong side row.
Cast off.

left front

With 5mm needles and C, cast on 40 (44: 48: 48: 52) sts.
1st row (right side) K2, * p2, k2; rep from * to last 6 sts, p2, k4.
2nd row * K2, p2; rep from * to end.
These 2 rows **form** the rib.
Change to M.
Cont in rib until front measures 14 (15: 17: 19: 22)cm from cast-on edge, ending with a wrong side row.
Shape armhole
Cast on 1 st at beg of next row. **41 (45: 49: 49: 53) sts.**
Working cast-on st as p1 on right side rows and k1 on wrong side rows, cont in rib as now set until front measures 22 (24: 24: 27: 29)cm from cast-on edge, ending with a wrong side row.
Buttonhole row Rib to last 4 sts, k2tog, yf, k2.
Shape neck
Next row Cast off 21 (24: 27: 26: 29) sts, patt to end.
Work straight in rib as set until front measures same as Back to shoulder, ending with a wrong side row.
Cast off.

right front

With 5mm needles and C, cast on 40 (44: 48: 48: 52) sts.
1st row (right side) K4, * p2, k2; rep from * to end.
2nd row P2, * k2, p2; rep from * to last 2 sts, k2.
These 2 rows **form** the rib.
Change to M.
Cont in rib until front measures 14 (15: 17: 19: 22)cm from cast-on edge, ending with a right side row.
Shape armhole
Cast on 1 st at beg of next row. **41 (45: 49: 49: 53) sts.**
Working cast on st as p1 on right side rows and k1 on wrong side rows, cont straight until front measures same as Back to shoulder, ending with a wrong side row.
Cast off.

sleeves	With 5mm needles and C, cast on 42 (46: 50: 54: 58) sts.

sleeves

With 5mm needles and C, cast on 42 (46: 50: 54: 58) sts.
1st row (right side) K2, * p2, k2; rep from * to end.
Change to M.
2nd row P2, * k2, p2; rep from * to end.
These 2 rows **form** the rib.
Work a further 6 rows.
Change to 4.50mm needles.
Work a further 8 rows.
Change to 5mm needles.
Cont in rib and inc 1 st at each end of the 5th and every foll 4th row until there are
52 (58: 64: 72: 76) sts.
Cont straight until sleeve measures 19 (21: 23: 25: 27)cm from cast-on edge, ending with a
wrong side row.
Cast off.

to make up

Join shoulder seams. Sew on sleeves. Join side and sleeve seams reversing seam for 5cm cuff.
Overlapping left front with right front, sew button to wrong side of right front to correspond
with buttonhole. Cut ribbon in half and sew one piece to right front edge and other piece onto
left front to match, then tie.

pinafore dress

measurements
To fit ages 3–6 (6–9: 9–12) months
finished measurements
Chest 47 (52: 57) cm
Length to shoulder 36 (42: 48) cm

materials
3 (4: 4) x 50g balls Debbie Bliss Baby Cashmerino in grey
Pair each 3 mm and 3.25 mm knitting needles
2 buttons

tension
25 sts and 40 rows to 10 cm over moss st using 3.25 mm needles.

abbreviations
See page 25.

front

With 3mm needles, cast on 101 (109: 117) sts.
Beg with a k row, work in st st.
Work 2 rows.
Eyelet row K1, * yf, k2tog; rep from * to end.
Work 3 rows.
Change to 3.25mm needles.
Moss st row K1, * p1, k1; rep from * to end.
This row **forms** the moss st and is repeated.
Cont straight in moss st until back measures 22 (26: 30) cm from cast-on edge, ending with a wrong-side row.
Dec row (right side) K1 (2: 4), [skpo, k1, k2tog] 20 (21: 22) times, k0 (2: 3). **61 (67: 73) sts.**
Change to 3mm needles. **
K 5 rows.
Cast off 8 (9: 10) sts at beg of next 2 garter st rows. **45 (49: 53) sts.**
Change to 3.25mm needles.
Next row K3, * p1, k1; rep from * to last 4 sts, p1, k3.
This row **forms** the moss st with garter st borders.
Patt 1 row.
Next row K2, skpo, patt to last 4 sts, k2tog, k2.
Patt 3 rows.
Rep the last 4 rows 6 (7: 8) times more. **31 (33: 35) sts.**
Patt 1 row.
Change to 3mm needles.
K 5 rows.
Straps
Next row (right side) K6, turn.
Work on these 6 sts only for first strap until strap measures 25 (27: 29) cm.
Cast off.
With right side facing, rejoin yarn to rem sts, cast off 19 (21: 23) sts, k to end.
Work on rem 6 sts for second strap until strap measures 25 (27: 29) cm.
Cast off.

back

Work as given for Front to **.
K 3 rows.
Buttonhole row K15 (17: 19), yf, k2tog, k to last 17 (19: 21) sts, k2tog, yf, k15 (17: 19).
K 3 rows.
Cast off.

to make up

Join side seams. Fold hem to wrong side and sew in place. Sew buttons to ends of straps to fit.

lacyshawl

size
94 x 110 cm, excluding edging

materials
16 x 50g balls Debbie Bliss Baby Cashmerino in pale blue
Pair 3.25mm knitting needles
3.25mm circular knitting needle

tension
24 sts and 40 rows to 10 cm square over centre lace patt using 3.25mm needles.

abbreviations
sk2togpo = sl 1, k2tog, pass slipped st over.
y2rn = yarn round needle twice to make 2 sts.
See page 25.

centre square

With 3.25mm circular needle, cast on 239 sts.

1st row (right side) K2, * k1 tbl, k2, yf, skpo, k4, yf, skpo, k3, k2tog, yf, k2; rep from * to last 3 sts, k1 tbl, k2.

2nd and every foll wrong-side row P.

3rd row K2, * k1, k2tog, yf, k1 tbl, yf, skpo; rep from * to last 3 sts, k3.

5th row K1, yf, * sk2togpo, yf, k3, yf; rep from * to last 4 sts, sk2togpo, yf, k1.

7th row K2, * yf, skpo, k3, k2tog, yf, k5, yf, skpo, k4; rep from * to last 3 sts, yf, skpo, k1.

9th row K2tog, yf, * k1 tbl, yf, skpo, k3, k1 tbl, k2, yf, skpo, k1, k1 tbl, k3, k2tog, yf; rep from * to last 3 sts, k1 tbl, yf, skpo.

11th row K2, * k2, yf, skpo, k3, k2tog, yf, k1 tbl, yf, skpo, k3, k2tog, yf, k1; rep from * to last 3 sts, k3.

13th row K2, * k3, yf, skpo, k1, k2tog, yf, k3, yf, skpo, k1, k2tog, yf, k2; rep from * to last 3 sts, k3.

15th row K2, * [yf, skpo, k2] twice, yf, sk2togpo, yf, k2, k2tog, yf, k3; rep from * to last 3 sts, yf, skpo, k1.

17th row K2tog, yf, * k1 tbl, [yf, skpo, k2] twice, yf, skpo, k1, k2tog, yf, k2, k2tog, yf; rep from * to last 3 sts, k1 tbl, yf, skpo.

19th row K2, * [k2, yf, skpo] twice, k1, k1 tbl, k1, k2tog, yf, k2, k2tog, yf, k1; rep from * to last 3 sts, k3.

21st row K1, yf, * sk2togpo, yf, k5, yf, skpo, k1, k2tog, yf, k5, yf; rep from * to last 4 sts, sk2togpo, yf, k1.

23rd row K2, * yf, skpo, k6, yf, sk2togpo, yf, k7; rep from * to last 3 sts, yf, skpo, k1.

24th row As 2nd row.

These 24 rows **form** the centre patt and are repeated.

Cont in patt ending with the 23rd row of the 17th patt repeat (407 rows worked).

Cast off.

edging

With 3.25mm needles, cast on 10 sts.

K 1 row, then work in patt as follows:

1st row (wrong side) Sl 1, [k1, yf, k2tog] twice, k1, y2rn, k1, y2rn, k1.

2nd row [K2, p1] twice (each y2rn is treated as 2 sts, the first is worked as k1, the second as p1), k2, [yf, k2tog, k1] twice.

3rd row Sl 1, [k1, yf, k2tog] twice, k7.

4th row Cast off 4, k3, [yf, k2tog, k1] twice.

These 4 rows **form** the border patt and are repeated until border is long enough to fit all around the edge of the centre patt, gathering slightly at the corners, ending with a 3rd row.

Cast off.

to make up

Block centre square by placing a towel over a board and pinning knitting out to the correct dimensions. Spray lightly with water and leave to dry. Cover border in sections with a damp cloth and press lightly with a medium iron. Join ends of edging across the cast-on and cast-off edges and sew around the edge of the square.

size
To fit age 3–6 months

materials
1 x 50g ball Debbie Bliss Baby Cashmerino in pale blue
Pair 2.75mm knitting needles
2 buttons

tension
28 sts and 37 rows to 10cm square over st st using 2.75mm needles.

abbreviations
See page 25.

sandals

right sandal

With 2.75mm needles, cast on 36 sts.

K 1 row.

1st row (right side) K1, yf, k16, yf, [k1, yf] twice, k16, yf, k1.

2nd and all wrong side rows K to end, working k1 tbl into each yf of previous row.

3rd row K2, yf, k16, yf, k2, yf, k3, yf, k16, yf, k2.

5th row K3, yf, k16, yf, [k4, yf] twice, k16, yf, k3.

7th row K4, yf, k16, yf, k5, yf, k6, yf, k16, yf, k4.

9th row K5, yf, k16, yf, [k7, yf] twice, k16, yf, k5.

11th row K22, yf, k8, yf, k9, yf, k22. **64 sts.**

12th row As 2nd row.

Beg with a k row, work 7 rows in st st.

Next row [P next st tog with corresponding st 7 rows below] to end.

Beg with a k row, work 8 rows in st st.

Shape instep

Next row K36, skpo, turn.

Next row Sl 1, p8, p2tog, turn.

Next row Sl 1, k8, skpo, turn.

Rep the last 2 rows 7 times more, then work the first of the 2 rows again.

Next row Sl 1, k to end.

Next row K17, k2tog, p8, skpo, k17. **44 sts.**

Next row K24, turn.

Next row P4, turn.

Next row K4, turn.

Work 6cm in st st on these 4 sts only for front strap.

Cast off these 4 sts.

With right side facing, rejoin yarn at base of strap, pick up and k15 sts along side edge of strap, then turn and cast off 26 sts knitwise, leave rem 9 sts on a holder.

With right side facing, rejoin yarn to top of other side of strap, pick up and k15 sts along side edge of strap, then k rem 20 sts.

Next row K9, cast off rem 26 sts knitwise.

Join sole and back heel seam.

With right side facing and 2.75mm needles, k across 18 sts along heel for ankle strap. **

Next row Cast on 22 sts, k to end, turn and cast on 4 sts.

Buttonhole row K to last 3 sts, yf, k2tog, k1.

K 2 rows.

Cast off.

Fold front strap over ankle strap and slip stitch cast-off edge in place.

Sew on button.

left sandal

Work as given for Right Sandal to **.

Next row Cast on 4 sts, k to end, turn and cast on 22 sts.

Buttonhole row K1, skpo, yf, k to end.

Complete as Right Sandal.

picot bootees

size
To fit age 3–6 months

materials
1 x 50g ball Debbie Bliss Baby Cashmerino in ecru
Pair 2.75mm knitting needles
2 buttons

tension
28 sts and 37 rows to 10cm square over st st using 2.75mm needles.

abbreviations
See page 25.

right bootee

With 2.75mm needles, cast on 36 sts.

K 1 row.

1st row (right side) K1, yf, k16, yf, [k1, yf] twice, k16, yf, k1.

2nd and all wrong side rows K to end, working k1 tbl into each yf of previous row.

3rd row K2, yf, k16, yf, k2, yf, k3, yf, k16, yf, k2.

5th row K3, yf, k16, yf, [k4, yf] twice, k16, yf, k3.

7th row K4, yf, k16, yf, k5, yf, k6, yf, k16, yf, k4.

9th row K5, yf, k16, yf, [k7, yf] twice, k16, yf, k5.

11th row K22, yf, k8, yf, k9, yf, k22. **64 sts.**

12th row As 2nd row.

K 12 rows.

Shape instep

Next row K36, skpo, turn.

Next row Sl 1, p8, p2tog, turn.

Next row Sl 1, k8, skpo, turn.

Rep the last 2 rows 5 times more, then work first of the 2 rows again.

Next row Sl 1, k to end.

Next row K19, k2tog, k8, skpo, k19. **48 sts.**

Next row K9, leave these sts on a holder, cast off one st, [slip the st now on right-hand needle back onto left-hand needle, cast on 2 sts, cast off 4 sts] 14 times, slip the st back onto left-hand needle, cast on 2 sts, cast off 3 sts, k to end, leave these 9 sts on a holder.

Join sole and back heel seam.

With wrong side facing and 2.75mm needles, k across 18 sts on holder for ankle strap. **

Next row Cast on 4 sts, k to end, turn and cast on 22 sts.

Buttonhole row K1, skpo, yf, k to end.

K 2 rows.

Cast off.

Sew on button.

left bootee

Work as given for Right Bootee to **.

Next row Cast on 22 sts, k to end, turn and cast on 4 sts.

Buttonhole row K to last 3 sts, yf, k2tog, k1.

Complete as Right Bootee.

size
To fit age 3–6 months

materials
1 x 50g ball Debbie Bliss Baby Cashmerino in teal
Pair 2.75mm knitting needles

tension
28 sts and 50 rows to 10cm square over garter st using 2.75mm needles.

abbreviations
See page 25.

baby bootees

to make

With 2.75mm needles, cast on 18 sts (for first half of cuff) and k 12 rows.
Break off yarn and leave these sts on a holder.
With 2.75mm needles, cast on 18 sts (for second half of cuff) and k 12 rows.
Join cuff halves
Next row [K1, p1] 9 times, then [k1, p1] 9 times across first half of cuff on holder. **36 sts.**
Next row [K1, p1] to end.
Rep the last row 6 times more.
Shape instep
Next row (RS) K23, turn.
Next row K10, turn.
Work 24 rows in garter st on centre 10 sts.
Next row K1, skpo, k4, k2tog, k1. **8 sts.**
K 1 row.
Cut yarn.
With RS facing, rejoin yarn at base of instep, pick up and k13 sts evenly along side of instep, k across centre 8 sts, then pick up and k13 sts evenly along other side of instep, k rem 13 sts. **60 sts.**
K 13 rows.
Beg with a k row, work 7 rows in st st.
Next row [P next st tog with corresponding st 7 rows below] to end.
Break off yarn.
Shape sole
Next row Slip first 25 sts onto right-hand needle, rejoin yarn and k10 sts, turn.
Next row K9, k2tog, turn.
Rep last row until 20 sts rem.
Cast off.

to make up

Join back seam. With back seam to centre of cast off, join heel seam.

laceedgecardigan

measurements

To fit ages 3–6 (6–9: 9–12: 12–18: 18–24) months

actual measurements

Chest 50 (54: 59: 62: 68)cm

Length to shoulder 22 (24: 26: 29: 32)cm

Sleeve length 15 (17: 19: 21: 23)cm

materials

3 (4: 4: 5: 6) x 50g balls Debbie Bliss Baby Cashmerino in pale pink

Pair 3.25mm knitting needles

tension

26 sts and 52 rows to 10cm square over garter st using 3.25mm needles.

abbreviations

kfb = knit into front and back of st.

See page 25.

back & fronts

Worked in one piece to armholes.
With 3.25mm needles, cast on 117 (127: 139: 149: 163) sts.
Work straight in garter st (knit every row) until work measures 12 (13: 14: 16: 18)cm from cast-on edge, ending with a right side row.

Divide for back and fronts
Next row K23 (25: 28: 31: 34), these sts will form left front, cast off 6 for left underarm, k until there are 59 (65: 71: 75: 83) sts on right needle, these sts will form the back, cast off 6 for right underarm, k to end.
Cont on last set of 23 (25: 28: 31: 34) sts for right front, place rem 2 groups of sts on holders.
Next row (right side) K5, skpo, k16 (18: 21: 24: 27).
K 3 rows.
Next row K5, skpo, k to end.
Rep the last 4 rows until 12 (13: 15: 16: 18) sts rem.
Cont straight until front measures 22 (24: 26: 29: 32)cm from cast-on edge, ending with a wrong side row.
Leave sts on a holder.

Left front
With right side facing, rejoin yarn to 23 (25: 28: 31: 34) sts held on holder for left front,
k16 (18: 21: 24: 27), k2tog, k5.
K 3 rows.
Rep the last 4 rows, working one less st before the dec each time, until 12 (13: 15: 16: 18) sts rem.
Cont straight until front measures 22 (24: 26: 29: 32)cm from cast-on edge, ending with a wrong side row.
Leave sts on a holder.

Back
With right side facing, rejoin yarn to 59 (65: 71: 75: 83) sts held on holder for back, k to end.
Cont straight until back measures 22 (24: 26: 29: 32)cm from cast-on edge, ending with a wrong side row.
Leave sts on needle.

sleeves

With 3.25mm needles, cast on 37 (40: 45: 48: 51) sts.
K 6 rows.
Inc row Kfb, k to last 2 sts, kfb, k1.
K 5 (6: 6: 7: 8) rows.
Rep the last 6 (7: 7: 8: 9) rows, 6 (7: 7: 8: 9) times more, then the inc row once more.
53 (58: 63: 68: 73) sts.
Work straight until sleeve measures 12 (14: 16: 18: 20)cm from cast-on edge.
Mark each end of last row, then k a further 6 rows.
Cast off.

to make up

With wrong side facing, slip 12 (13: 15: 16: 18) sts of left front onto a 3.25mm needle, then with wrong side facing slip 12 (13: 15: 16: 18) sts of right front onto same needle, needle will be

pointing towards right armhole. With right sides of Fronts and Back together, cast off shoulder sts working one st of right front and one st of back together each time. When all right front sts have been cast off, cont to cast off sts of Back until 12 (13: 15: 16: 18) sts rem on left hand needle and 1 st rems on right hand needle, now cast off left front and back sts together as before.

Join sleeve seams, leaving seam open above markers.

Sew sleeves into armholes, with cast-off edge sewn to row-ends of armhole and row-ends of sleeve sewn to cast-off sts of underarm.

edgings

With 3.25mm needles, cast on 5 sts.

1st row (right side) K1, yf, k2tog, yf, k2.

2nd, 4th, 6th and 8th rows Knit.

3rd row K2, yf, k2tog, yf, k2.

5th row K3, yf, k2tog, yf, k2.

7th row K4, yf, k2tog, yf, k2.

9th row K5, yf, k2tog, yf, k2.

10th row Cast off 5 sts, k to end. 5 sts.

These 10 rows **form** the lace edging and are repeated throughout.

Cuff edging (make 2)

Work reps of the 10 row patt until edging fits along lower edge of sleeve, ending with a 10th row. Cast off rem 5 sts.

Front and neck edging

Work reps of the 10 row patt until edging fits along left front edge, around back neck and down right front edge, ending with a 10th row. Cast off rem 5 sts.

Stitch edging around front and and neck edges and around sleeve edges.

roll edge jacket 275

measurements
To fit ages 3–6 (6–9: 9–12: 12–18: 18–24) months
actual measurements
Chest 48 (54: 60: 66: 72)cm
Length to shoulder 33 (35: 37: 38: 41)cm
Sleeve length 14 (16: 18: 20: 22)cm

materials
6 (7: 8: 9: 10) x 50g balls Debbie Bliss Cotton Double Knitting in chocolate (M)
and 1 x 50g ball in duck egg blue (C)
Pair 4mm knitting needles
3 buttons

tension
20 sts and 39 rows to 10cm square over garter st using 4mm needles.

abbreviations
See page 25.

back

With 4mm needles and C, cast on 66 (72: 78: 84: 90) sts.
Beg with a k row, work 3 rows in st st.
Change to M and p 1 row.
K 6 (6: 8: 8: 8) rows.
Next row (right side) K6, skpo, k to last 8 sts, k2tog, k6.
K 1 row.
Rep the last 8 (8: 10: 10: 10) rows, 7 times more. **50 (56: 62: 68: 74)** sts.
K 8 (12: 0: 4: 8) rows.
Shape armholes
Cast off 3 (3: 4: 4: 5) sts at beg of next 2 rows. **44 (50: 54: 60: 64)** sts.
K 2 rows.
Next row (right side) K2, skpo, k to last 4 sts, k2tog, k2.
K 3 rows.
Rep the last 4 rows 9 (10: 11: 12: 13) times more. **24 (28: 30: 34: 36)** sts.
Leave sts on a holder.

left front

With 4mm needles and C, cast on 35 (38: 41: 44: 47) sts.
Beg with a k row, work 3 rows in st st.
Change to M and p 1 row.
K 6 (6: 8: 8: 8) rows.
Next row (right side) K6, skpo, k to end.
K 1 row.
Rep the last 8 (8: 10: 10: 10) rows, 7 times more. **27 (30: 33: 36: 39)** sts.
K 8 (12: 0: 4: 8) rows.
Shape armhole
Cast off 3 (3: 4: 4: 5) sts at beg of next row. **24 (27: 29: 32: 34)** sts.
K 3 rows.
Next row (right side) K2, skpo, k to end.
K 3 rows.
Rep the last 4 rows 3 (3: 3: 3: 4) times more. **20 (23: 25: 28: 29)** sts.
Next row (right side) K2, skpo, k to end.
K 0 (0: 2: 2: 0) rows.
Shape neck
Next row (wrong side) Cast off 4 sts, k to end.
1st, 2nd and 5th sizes only
Next row K to last 4 sts, k2tog, k2.
K 1 row.
All sizes
Next row K2, skpo, k to last 4 sts, k2tog, k2.
K 1 row.
Next row K to last 4 sts, k2tog, k2.
K 1 row.
Rep the last 4 rows 1 (2: 3: 4: 4) times more. **8** sts.
Next row K2, skpo, k2tog, k2. **6** sts.

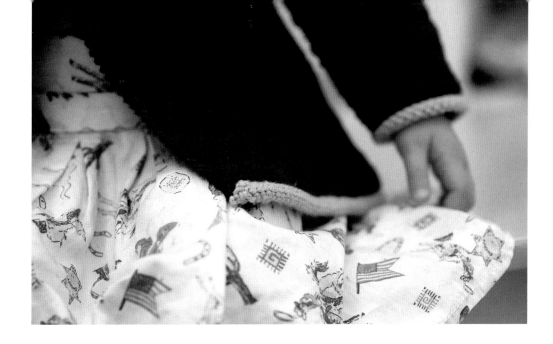

K 3 rows.
Next row K1, skpo, k2tog, k1. **4 sts.**
K 3 rows.
Next row Skpo, k2tog. **2 sts.**
K 3 rows.
Leave rem sts on a safety pin.

right front

With 4mm needles and C, cast on 35 (38: 41: 44: 47) sts.
Beg with a k row, work 3 rows in st st.
Change to M and p 1 row.
K 6 (6: 8: 8: 8) rows.
Next row (right side) K to last 8 sts, k2tog, k6.
K 1 row.
Rep the last 8 (8: 10: 10: 10) rows, 6 (6: 5: 5: 5) times more. 28 (31: 35: 38: 41) sts.
K 2 (2: 4: 4: 6) rows.
1st buttonhole row (right side) K2, yf, k2tog, k to end.
K 3 (3: 3: 3: 1) rows.
Next row (right side) K to last 8 sts, k2tog, k6. 27 (30: 34: 37: 40) sts.
3rd, 4th and 5th sizes only
K 9 rows.
Next row (right side) K to last 8 sts, k2tog, k6.
All sizes
K 10 (13: 2: 5: 9) rows.
2nd, 4th and 5th sizes only
2nd buttonhole row (right side): K2, yf, k2tog, k to end.
All sizes

Shape armhole

Next row (wrong side) Cast off 3 (3: 4: 4: 5) sts, k to end. **24 (27: 29: 32: 34) sts.**

1st and 3rd sizes only

2nd buttonhole row (right side) K2, yf, k2tog, k to end.

All sizes

K 1 (2: 1: 2: 2) rows.

Next row (right side) K to last 4 sts, k2tog, k2.

K 3 rows.

Rep the last 4 rows 2 (2: 3: 3: 3) times more. **21 (24: 25: 28: 30) sts.**

1st, 2nd and 5th sizes only

Next row (right side) K to last 4 sts, k2tog, k2.

K 1 row.

3rd buttonhole row (right side) K2, yf, k2tog, k to end.

K 1 row.

Next row K to last 4 sts, k2tog, k2.

K 1 row.

Shape neck

Next row (right side) Cast off 4 sts, with 1 st on needle, k1, skpo, k to end.

K 1 row.

Next row K2, skpo, k to last 4 sts, k2tog, k2.

K 1 row.

Next row K2, skpo, k to end.

K 1 row.

3rd and 4th sizes only

3rd buttonhole row (right side) K2, yf, k2tog, k to last 4 sts, k2tog, k2.

K 3 rows.

Shape neck

Next row (right side) Cast off 4 sts, with 1 st on needle, k1, skpo, k to last 4 sts, k2tog, k2.

K 1 row.

Next row (right side) K2, skpo, k to end.

K 1 row.

Next row K2, skpo, k to last 4 sts, k2tog, k2.

K 1 row.

Next row (right side) K2, skpo, k to end.

K 1 row.

All sizes

Rep the last 4 rows 1 (2: 2: 3: 4) times more. **8 sts.**

Next row K2, skpo, k2tog, k2. **6 sts.**

K 3 rows.

Next row K1, skpo, k2tog, k1. **4 sts.**

K 3 rows.

Next row Skpo, k2tog. **2 sts.**

K 3 rows.

Leave rem sts on a safety pin.

sleeves

With 4mm needles and C, cast on 28 (30: 32: 32: 34) sts.

Beg with a k row, work 3 rows in st st.

Change to M and p 1 row.

Now work in garter st and inc 1 st at each end of 7th (11th: 11th: 11th: 11th) and every foll 8th row until there are 40 (42: 46: 48: 52) sts.

Cont straight until sleeve measures 13 (15: 17: 19: 21)cm from start of garter st, ending with a wrong side row.

Shape raglans

Cast off 3 (3: 4: 4: 5) sts at beg of next 2 rows. **34 (36: 38: 40: 42) sts.**

K 2 rows.

Next row K2, skpo, k to last 4 sts, k2tog, k2.

K 3 rows.

Rep the last 4 rows 3 (4: 5: 6: 7) times more. **26 sts.**

Next row K2, skpo, k7, skpo, k2tog, k7, k2tog, k2.

K 3 rows.

Next row K2, skpo, k to last 4 sts, k2tog, k2. **20 sts.**

K 3 rows.

Next row K2, skpo, k4, skpo, k2tog, k4, k2tog, k2.

K 3 rows.

Next row K2, skpo, k to last 4 sts, k2tog, k2. **14 sts.**

K 3 rows.

Next row K2, skpo, k1, skpo, k2tog, k1, k2tog, k2.

K 3 rows.

Next row K2, skpo, k to last 4 sts, k2tog, k2. **8 sts.**

K 3 rows.

Leave rem 8 sts on a holder.

collar

Join raglan seams.

With right side facing, 4mm needles and M, beg 2 sts in from front edge, pick up and k13 (15: 15: 17: 19) sts up right front neck, k2tog from safety pin, work [k2tog, k4, k2tog] across 8 sts of right sleeve, work [k2tog, k5 (6: 7: 8: 8), k2tog, k6 (8: 8: 10: 12), k2tog, k5 (6: 7: 8: 8), k2tog] across 24 (28: 30: 34: 36) sts on back neck holder, work [k2tog, k4, k2tog] across sts of left sleeve, k2tog from safety pin, then pick up and k14 (16: 16: 18: 20) sts down left front neck, ending 2 sts in from front edge. **61 (69: 71: 79: 85) sts.**

1st row (wrong side) K all sts.

Change to C.

Beg with a k row, work 7 rows in st st.

Cast off.

to make up

Join side and sleeve seams, reversing seam on contrast edges, allowing these to roll.

Sew on buttons.

yarndistributors

For stockists of Debbie Bliss yarns please contact:

UK & WORLDWIDE DISTRIBUTORS
Designer Yarns Ltd
Units 8–10
Newbridge Industrial Estate
Pitt Street, Keighley
West Yorkshire BD21 4PQ
UK
t: +44 (0) 1535 664222
f: +44 (0) 1535 664333
e: alex@designeryarns.uk.com
w: www.designeryarns.uk.com

USA
Knitting Fever Inc.
315 Bayview Avenue
Amityville
NY 11701
USA
t: +1 516 546 3600
f: +1 516 546 6871
w: www.knittingfever.com

AUSTRALIA/NEW ZEALAND
Prestige Yarns Pty Ltd
PO Box 39
Bulli
NSW 2516
Australia
t: +61 (0) 2 4285 6669
e: info@prestigeyarns.com
w: www.prestigeyarns.com

BRAZIL
Quatro Estacoes Com
Las Linhas e Acessorios Ltda
Av. Das Nacoes Unidas
12551-9 Andar
Cep 04578-000 Sao Paulo
Brazil
t: +55 11 3443 7736
e: cristina@4estacoeslas.com.br

CANADA
Diamond Yarns Ltd
155 Martin Ross Avenue, Unit 3
Toronto
Ontario M3J 2L9
Canada
t: +1 416 736 6111
f: +1 416 736 6112
w: www.diamondyarn.com

DENMARK
Fancy Knit
Hovedvejen 71
8586 Oerum Djurs
Ramten
Denmark
t: +45 59 46 21 89
f: +45 59 46 80 18
e: roenneburg@mail.dk

FINLAND
Eiran Tukku
Mäkeländkatu 54 B
00510 Helsinki
Finland
t: +358 50 346 0575
e: maria.hellbom@eirantukku.fi

FRANCE
Plassard Diffusion
La Filature
71800 Varennes-sous-Dun
France
t: +33 (0) 3 85282828
f: +33 (0) 3 85282829
e: info@laines-plassard.com

GERMANY/AUSTRIA/
SWITZERLAND/LUXEMBOURG/
BELGIUM/HOLLAND
Designer Yarns (Deutschland) GmbH
Welserstrasse 10g
D-51149 Köln
Germany
t: +49 (0) 2203 1021910
f: +49 (0) 2203 1023551
e: info@designeryarns.de
w: www.designeryarns.de

HONG KONG
East Unit Company
Unit B2, 7/F Block B
Kailey Industrial Centre
12 Fung Zip Street
Chan Wan
Hong Kong
t: +852 2869 7110
f: +852 2537 6952
e: eastunity@yahoo.com.hk

ICELAND
Storkurinn Ehf
Laugavegi 59
101 Reykjavik
Iceland
t: +354 551 8258
f: +354 562 8252
e: storkurinn@simnet.is

MEXICO
Estambres Crochet SA de CV
Aaron Saenz 1891-7
Col. Santa Maria
Monterrey
N.L. 64650
Mexico
t: +52 (81) 8335 3870
e: abremer@redmundial.com.mx

NORWAY
Viking of Norway
Bygdaveien 63
4333 Oltedal
Norway
t: +47 516 11 660
f: +47 516 16 235
e: post@viking-garn.no
w: www.viking-garn.no

RUSSIA
Golden Fleece Ltd
Soloviyny Proezd 16
117593 Moscow
Russian Federation
Russia
t: +8 (903) 000 1967
e: natalya@rukodelie.ru
w: www.rukodelie.ru

SPAIN
Oyambre Needlework SL
Balmes, 200 At. 4
08006 Barcelona
Spain
t: +34 (0) 93 487 26 72
f: +34 (0) 93 218 66 94
e: info@oyambreonline.com

SWEDEN
Nysta Garn Och Textil
Hogasvagen 20
S-131 47 Nacka
Sweden
t: +46 708 81 39 54
e: info@nysta.se
w: www.nysta.se

TAIWAN
U-Knit
1F, 199-1 Sec
Zhong Xiao East Road
Taipei
Taiwan
t: +886 2 275 275 57
f: +886 2 275 285 56
e: shuindigo@hotmail.com

THAILAND
Needle World Co Ltd
Pradit Manoontham Road
Bangkok 10310
Thailand
t: +662 933 9167
f: +662 933 9110
e: needle-
world.coltd@googlemail.com

For more information on my
other books and yarns, please
visit www.debbieblissonline.com

index

acknowledgements

This book wouldn't have been possible without the generous collaboration of the following:

Rosy Tucker, who produced all the wonderful toys. Her practical and creative input is always invaluable. Also for the pattern checking.

Penny Hill, for her essential pattern compiling and organising the knitters.

Jane O'Shea, **Lisa Pendreigh** and **Mary Evans** at Quadrille Publishing for being such a wonderful team to work with.

Julie Mansfield for the perfect styling and overall look.

Tim Evan-Cook, **Ulla Nyeman** and **Debi Treloar** for the beautiful photography.

Sally Kvalheim and **Jo Gillingwater** for the great job baby grooming.

And, of course, the fantastic mothers and babies: **Alara**, **Anwyn**, **Casey** and **Evelyn**, **Charlie**, **Conor**, **Daisy**, **Dotty**, **Dylan**, **Frankie**, **Funsho** and **Levi**, **Grace**, **Guy**, **Hayden**, **Jago**, **Jake**, **Katherine**, **Kristina**, **Laud**, **Luca**, **Luna**, **Mathilda**, **Mimi**, **Monty**, **Noah**, **Rachel** and **Joshua**, **Reggie**, **Robyn**, **Rosie** and **Sydney**.

The knitters, for the huge effort they put into creating perfect knits under deadline pressure: **Cynthia Brent**, **Barbara Clapham**, **Pat Church**, **Jacqui Dunt**, **Shirley Kennet**, **Maisie Lawrence** and **Frances Wallace**.

My fantastic agent, **Heather Jeeves**.

The distributors, **agents**, **retailers** and **knitters** who support all my books and yarns with such enthusiasm and make what I do possible.

Editorial Director **Jane O'Shea**
Creative Director **Mary Evans**
Project Editor **Lisa Pendreigh**
Photographers **Tim Evan-Cook, Ulla Nyeman and Debi Treloar**
Stylist **Julie Mansfield**
Illustrator **Kate Simunek**
Pattern Illustrator **Bridget Bodoano**
Production Director **Vincent Smith**
Production Controller **Ruth Deary**

First published in 2011 by
Quadrille Publishing Limited
Alhambra House
27–31 Charing Cross Road
London WC2H 0LS
www.quadrille.co.uk

Based on material originally published in **Simply Baby**, **Essential Baby** and **Blankets, Bears and Bootees**

Text and project designs © 2006, 2007, 2009 Debbie Bliss
Photography, design and layout © 2006, 2007, 2009 Quadrille
Publishing Limited

British Library Cataloguing-in-Publication Data
A catalogue record for this book is available from the British Library.

ISBN: 978 184400 945 9

Printed in China

Photo credits
Tim Evan-Cook: pages 4, 6–13, 26–28; 40–45, 62–67, 80–95, 108–109, 114–123, 148–153, 162–167, 174–177, 182–197, 206– 213, 232–237, 248–251, 270–280 and 284–286.
Ulla Nyeman: pages 5, 33–35, 52–61, 110–113, 136–147; 218–231, 238–247, 260–269, 281–283 and 288.
Debi Treloar: pages 3, 14–25, 29–32, 36–39, 46–51, 68–79, 96–107, 124–135, 154–161, 168–173, 178–181, 198–205, 214–217 and 252–259.